PANZER 38(t)
VS
BT-7

Barbarossa 1941

STEVEN J. ZALOGA

First published in Great Britain in 2017 by Osprey Publishing,
PO Box 883, Oxford, OX1 9PL, UK
1385 Broadway, 5th Floor, New York, NY 10018, USA
E-mail: info@ospreypublishing.com

Osprey Publishing, part of Bloomsbury Publishing Plc

OSPREY is a trademark of Osprey Publishing, a division of Bloomsbury
Publishing Plc.

A CIP catalogue record for this book is available from the British Library.

Print ISBN: 978 1 4728 1713 6
PDF e-book ISBN: 978 1 4728 1714 3
ePub e-book ISBN: 978 1 4728 1715 0

Index by Rob Munro
Typeset in ITC Conduit and Adobe Garamond
Maps by bounford.com
Originated by PDQ Media, Bungay, UK
Printed in China through World Print Ltd.

17 18 19 20 21   10 9 8 7 6 5 4 3 2 1

Osprey Publishing supports the Woodland Trust, the UK's leading woodland
conservation charity. Between 2014 and 2018 our donations are being spent
on their Centenary Woods project in the UK.

To find out more about our authors and books visit **www.ospreypublishing.
com**. Here you will find extracts, author interviews, details of forthcoming
events and the option to sign up for our newsletter.

Author's note

The author would especially like to thank John Prigent and Wojceich Łuczak
for their help in obtaining photographs and other material for this book.
Unless otherwise noted, photographs are from the author's collection.

Title-page photograph: A BT-7 Model 1937 on parade before the war. The
rectangular containers on the trackguards are external fuel cells, each of the
four containing 32 litres. These were not connected to the internal fuel tank,
and had to be pumped into the main tank.

Glossary

Abt	*Abteilung*: unit between regiment and battalion (German)
Ausf	*Ausführung*: version (German)
BMM	Böhmisch-Mährische Maschinenfabrik AG: Bohemia-Moravia Industrial Plant, German name for ČKD
BT	*Bystrokhodny tank*: fast tank (Russian)
ČKD	Českomoravská-Kolben-Daněk (Czech)
DT	*Degtyarev tankoviy*: Degtyarev tank machine gun (Russian)
(f)	*französischen*: French (German)
Hauptmann	Captain (German)
Heeresgruppe	Army group (German): a formation with several field armies
Heereswaffenamt	Army Weapons Department (German)
KhT	*Khimicheskiy tank*: chemical (flamethrower) tank (Russian)
LT	Lehký Tank: light tank (Czech)
(mot.)	*motorisiert*: motorized (German)
Oberst	Colonel (German)
Oberstleutnant	Lieutenant-colonel (German)
OKH	Oberkommando des Heeres: Army High Command (German)
PzBefWg	*Panzerbefehlswagen*: armoured command vehicle (German)
PzgrPatr	*Panzergranate Patronen*: anti-tank round (German)
PzKpfw	*Panzerkampfwagen*: armoured combat vehicle; tank (German)
PzSpWg	*Panzerspähwagen*: armoured scout vehicle; armoured car (German)
(t)	*tschechoslowakischen*: Czechoslovak (German)
vz.	*Vzor*: model (Czech)

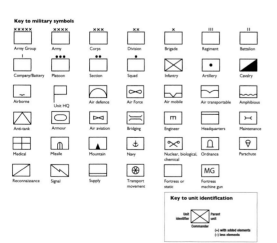

CONTENTS

INTRODUCTION

The largest tank battles in history took place as part of Operation *Barbarossa* during June–August 1941 in the western border region of the Soviet Union, with more than 13,000 Soviet tanks pitted against 3,400 German tanks. In spite of the Red Army's enormous quantitative advantage, its tank units were smashed in a series of violent confrontations. Nearly 12,000 Soviet tanks were lost in less than three weeks of

The PzKpfw 38(t) tanks carried a variety of logs, fascines and other engineer support material at the start of Operation *Barbarossa* to assist in crossing anti-tank ditches and other obstacles such as irrigation ditches. This is a tank of 11./PzRgt 25 at the start of the campaign. (John Prigent)

OPPOSITE A BT-7 Model 1937 with the P-40 anti-aircraft machine-gun mount, knocked out or abandoned in the Alytus (Olita) area after the 22 June battle. There is no battle damage evident, and this tank may have been abandoned and pushed off the road. (NARA)

combat; German tank losses were about 400. Recent Russian accounts have called these battles 'the great tank massacre of 1941'. Why were the Soviet tank losses so high?

To answer this question, this book focuses on the tank battles along the Neman (Nemunas) River in the Baltic region fought between Germany's 7. Panzer-Division and the Soviet Union's 5th Tank Division during the first few days of the conflict. These battles were chosen for several reasons. To begin with, there is enough documentation to provide a detailed description of the battles. From the German side, this book is based on the *Kriegstagebuch* (war diary) of 7. Panzer-Division as well as records of higher corps and army commands. There are no known records of the 5th Tank Division for this battle since the unit headquarters was destroyed and the vast majority of its troops killed or captured. In recent years, however, Russian researchers have uncovered extensive pre-war records of the 5th Tank Division that help provide a detailed picture of the unit's formation and training. There are also a handful of short accounts by a few surviving tankers of the 5th Tank Division in various Russian histories. Another reason for selecting this battle is a surviving photographic record of the battle. Record Group 242-GAP at the National Archives and Records Administration in the United States has a small collection of photographs of this battle that are especially valuable since they are clearly labelled regarding the date and location of the photographs, and in some cases even the time of day they were taken. The vast majority of surviving Operation *Barbarossa* photographs lack information on dates and location.

The two tank types that are the focus of this work are the German PzKpfw 38(t) and the Soviet BT-7. Both types were comparable in technical terms with similar levels of armour and firepower, making them a reasonably close technical match. Many histories of Operation *Barbarossa* deprecate the Soviet tanks as old and obsolete, other than the new T-34 medium and KV heavy tanks. This was not the case, and the BT-7 was clearly better than the majority of German tanks such as the PzKpfw I, PzKpfw II and PzKpfw 35(t). On the other hand, the BT-7 was inferior to German medium tanks such as the PzKpfw III and PzKpfw IV. Hence the choice of opposing tank types.

This crew of a BT-7 of the 2nd Tank Division (3rd Mechanized Corps) consists of the tank commander, Senior Sergeant N. Ananin (right), turret gunner Private S. Kashekin (above), and driver Corporal F. Lazarev (left).

Traditional assessments of tank performance centre on the 'holy trinity' of tank design: armour, firepower and mobility. However, a deeper assessment of tank effectiveness in battle must include less obvious factors such as tank reliability, tank command and control, and the situational awareness of the tank commander made possible by such features as vision devices and radio. Beyond the actual technical features of the tanks, the human element of tank combat is the predominant factor in the success or failure of tank combat. The importance of crew training, crew experience, unit training and unit tactics cannot be overemphasized.

An iconic portrait of a PzKpfw 38(t) crewman of 7. Panzer-Division, taken on 4 July 1940 in France. The padded Panzer beret, the *Schutzmütze*, was officially abandoned in favour of a field cap on 15 January 1941, though an exception was made for crews of the PzKpfw 38(t) due to the tank's cramped interior. In practice, most PzKpfw 38(t) crews had switched to the field cap by the time of Operation *Barbarossa*. (NARA)

The tanks of the Blitzkrieg era of 1939–41 were remarkably similar to the original tanks of World War I in some respects, yet surprisingly different in others. For the vast majority of tanks, tank armour was not that much better than in 1918: their armour plate was only sufficient to stop light-machine-gun fire. Firepower was not much better than the 37mm and 57mm guns commonplace on World War I tanks. Mobility was much improved, with most tanks capable of cross-country speeds of 25km/h compared to the arthritic walking speeds of most World War I tanks.

One of the most important but overlooked advances between 1918 and 1941 was in the matter of tank durability. World War I tanks were mechanically fragile – some of the German and French tanks could operate for only a day or two before having to be returned to depot for mechanical rebuilding. Even the more robust British tanks such as the Mark IV needed their tracks replacing after about 30km of travel. The most modern of the World War I tanks, the Renault FT light tank, was mechanically exhausted after 130km of travel and ready for the scrapyard. Most tank units in 1918 lost half or more of their tanks on the first day of combat due to mechanical problems. Early tanks were akin to siege engines: suitable for cracking open a trench line, but too mechanically exhausted to conduct persistent mobile operations. Tanks did not become a revolutionary tool of mobile warfare until tank designers managed to improve greatly their mechanical reliability. The tanks described in this book were among the first generation capable of carrying out sustained mobile operations lasting a few days or more. Even then, there were distinct limits to their durability, as will become apparent in this book.

One technical issue is worth discussing at the outset. The battles described here took part in Europe's 'shatter-zone' where borders changed frequently in the 20th century. As a result, the towns and rivers have Lithuanian, Polish, Russian and German names. Deciding on which geographic name to employ can be a bit tricky. The contemporary Lithuanian names might seem the most obvious choice, but they are often significantly different from the German and Russian names familiar to most military-history readers already acquainted with Operation *Barbarossa*. As a result, I have appended the more familiar names in this account, though contemporary Lithuanian names are used where appropriate.

CHRONOLOGY

1930

April J. Walter Christie signs a contract to provide two tanks plus licensed-production rights to the Soviet Union.

1931

May The BT-2 is accepted for production.

1933

January Production starts on the BT-5 tank.

1934

November The Red Army orders the BT-7 tank.

1938

August The Czechoslovak Army orders the LT vz. 38 tank.

September Germany takes the Sudetenland from Czechoslovakia.

1939

March Germany occupies the remainder of the Czech provinces.

March Germany takes the Klaipeda region from Lithuania.

May The first batch of LT vz. 38 is accepted for German service.

July BMM receives a second production contract for 325 PzKpfw 38(t) tanks.

1 September World War II begins with the German invasion of Poland.

17 September The Soviet Union invades Poland.

10 October The Soviet Union demands Lithuania permit the basing of Red Army units on its soil.

30 November The Soviet Union invades Finland.

A preserved example of the BT-7 Model 1935 at the Central Armed Forces Museum in Moscow.

1940

January — The standard designation PzKpfw 38(t) replaces the interim PzKpfw III(t) and Ltm 38 Protektorat.

February — 3. leichte Division is converted into 7. Panzer-Division.

10 May — Germany invades the Low Countries and begins its attack on France.

June — The Soviet Union's 3rd Mechanized Corps begins to be formed in Lithuania.

16 June — The Soviet Union takes the first steps to incorporate Lithuania into the Soviet Union.

November — Production begins of the PzKpfw 38(t) Ausf E with upgraded armour.

1941

22 June — Germany initiates Operation *Barbarossa*, the invasion of the Soviet Union.

22 June — At about 1245hrs, 7. Panzer-Division captures both bridges at Alytus (Olita) in Lithuania.

24 June — 7. Panzer-Division occupies Vilnius.

25 June — Remnants of the 5th Tank Division attack spearheads of 7. Panzer-Division along the road between Vilnius and Molodechno (now Maladzyechna, Belarus).

26 June — 7. Panzer-Division reaches Minsk as part of the German operation to encircle the Soviet Western Front.

DESIGN AND DEVELOPMENT

PzKpfw 38(t)

The PzKpfw 38(t) was the only tank of foreign origin to remain in production for the Wehrmacht through World War II. When Germany occupied the Czech provinces in 1939, it inherited the small but sophisticated Czech tank industry. The best of the new Czech tanks, the LT 38, was an essential element in enlarging the Panzer force in the Blitzkrieg years of 1939–41. German light tanks were armed with machine guns and 2cm cannon, but the Czech tanks offered an excellent 37mm gun, comparable to that on the PzKpfw III medium tank.

Czechoslovakia played an unusually significant role in European weapons production because the Czech lands had long been a major weapons centre for the Austro-Hungarian Empire. The Czechoslovak Army did not provide a large enough market to sustain these industries, so the focus shifted to the international export market. By the 1930s, there were two Czechoslovak firms involved in the tank-making business: the well-known armament firm Škoda in Pilsen (now Plzeň, Czech Republic) and the newcomer, ČKD, formed in Prague. Curiously enough, the principal design engineer at ČKD was an émigré Russian, Alexej Surin, who had migrated to Czechoslovakia in the wake of the Russian Civil War. One of Surin's technological innovations was a large road-wheel suspension system that offered a better ride than earlier types of spring suspension. Surin's large road-wheels might be mistaken for a Christie-type suspension such as those on the Soviet BT tanks, but in fact the Surin

design used a bogie consisting of twin road-wheels pivoting on a single horizontal spring rather than the individual vertical springs of the famous Christie design.

Development of the PzKpfw 38(t) can be traced back to Surin's work on the TNH light tank that competed against the Vickers 6-ton tank in the international arms-export market. Iran placed an order for 50 Czech tanks in 1935 and they were delivered in 1937. Variations of this design won further contracts including a Latvian order for 21 LTL tanks in 1937, a Peruvian order for 24 LTP tanks in 1938 and a Swiss order for the LTL-H, also known as the Panzerwagen 39 (Pzw 39).

ČKD's improved TNH-S design was accepted for Czechoslovak Army service as the LT vz. 38 on 31 August 1938. To drive down costs, ČKD received government approval to export the type even before series production had begun. The original prototype was shipped to Britain in February 1939 for trials by the War Mechanisation Board, but any potential sale was cancelled in June 1939 after the German occupation of Czech territory. Sweden also planned to order the type, though political events interfered as described below. Following the Munich agreement of 30 September 1938, Czechoslovakia was forced to relinquish the Sudetenland to Germany, including its elaborate line of fortifications along the border. On 15 March 1939, Germany occupied the remainder of the Czech provinces under a nominal 'Protectorate of Bohemia

A column from 3./PzAbt 67 (3. leichte Division) in Poland during September 1939. In the lead is a PzKpfw 38(t) Ausf A, followed by one of the rare PzKpfw II Ausf D.

and Moravia' and permitted the Slovak region to break off as an independent Slovak Republic.

The Czechoslovak Army's original plans expected the completion of all 150 LT vz. 38 tanks on order by March 1939, but in the event, none were received by the Czechoslovak Army prior to the German occupation. In May 1939, a German delegation from the Heereswaffenamt visited ČKD as part of a German programme to assess the future role of the Czech armament industry within the Reich. At the time, ten completed LT vz. 38 tanks were in the factory yards. The remaining 140 tanks from the Czechoslovak Army order were in various stages of construction. The German officers were impressed with the new tanks, mainly because of their excellent 37mm armament. At the time, German production of the PzKpfw III with a comparable 37mm gun had been continually delayed, and there was a desperate need for tanks with a good anti-tank armament. The vast majority of German tanks at the time were the PzKpfw I with twin 7.92mm machine guns and the PzKpfw II with a 20mm cannon, neither of which was adequate in fighting against modern tanks. The LT vz. 38 had the firepower of the PzKpfw III, but was closer in size and weight to the PzKpfw II light tank. The ČKD company was taken over by German management and was renamed as BMM to continue LT vz. 38 production for the German armed forces, the Wehrmacht. In January 1940, the designation PzKpfw 38(t) was introduced for this tank in favour of the previous and confusing designation PzKpfw III(t). Although the Heereswaffenamt was not especially enthusiastic about accepting foreign designs, the Czech industrial capacity was an attractive short-cut to building up the Panzer force quickly.

The Czechoslovak LT 35 and LT 38 tanks were primarily used in the mechanization of German cavalry. When the war started in Europe on 1 September 1939, a total of 78 PzKpfw 38(t) had been delivered and were assigned to Panzer-Abteilung 67 of the new 3. leichte Division, this being one of Germany's new mechanized-cavalry

PzKpfw 38(t) Ausf D, 7. PANZER-DIVISION

Crew: 4
Weight: 9.8 tonnes
Length: 4.61m
Width: 2.14m
Height: 2.25m
Main gun: 3.7cm KwK 38(t) gun
Main gun ammunition: 90 rounds 3.7cm
Secondary armament: Two 7.92mm MG 37(t); 1 machine
   gun on platoon command tanks
Machine-gun ammunition: 2,700 rounds 7.92mm
Radio: Fu 5 and Fu 2 transceiver (platoon commander)

Hull front armour: 25mm
Hull side armour: 15mm
Turret front armour: 25mm
Maximum speed: 42km/h
Cross-country speed (track): 15km/h
Road range: 250km
Terrain range: 100km
Fuel capacity: 220 litres
Engine type: Praga TNHPS/II
Transmission: Praga-Wilson CV
Horsepower: 125

4.61m

2.25m

2.14m

The PzKpfw 38(t) Ausf B incorporated changes to better integrate the design into German practices, including German radios and tools. This is a column from I./PzRgt 25 (7. Panzer-Division) in France during June 1940. (NARA)

divisions. 3. leichte Division saw combat with Heeresgruppe Süd on the southern front in Poland, including the Bzura River battles. Total losses were 6–7 tanks, with many others damaged. The knocked-out tanks were later rebuilt.

The Polish campaign made it obvious that the armour of the PzKpfw 38(t) was inadequate. The Polish Army had been amply equipped with 7.9mm wz.35 anti-tank rifles and 37mm wz.36 anti-tank guns. The anti-tank rifle could penetrate the frontal armour of the PzKpfw 38(t) at ranges of about 100m, and could penetrate the sides at ranges of 300m. In addition, the Polish Bofors 37mm anti-tank gun could penetrate the PzKpfw 38(t) at any normal combat range. This protective defect was not unique to the Czech tank design, and was a common problem with all of the German tanks of this era. From an organizational standpoint, the Polish campaign made it obvious that the Panzer division was more combat-effective than the mechanized-cavalry divisions. As a result, the four mechanized-cavalry divisions were rebuilt as Panzer divisions prior to the 1940 campaigns. This included 2. leichte Division which became 7. Panzer-Division, the focus of the actions described in this book.

By the time of the 1940 campaign in Western Europe, over 200 PzKpfw 38(t) tanks had been delivered and Czech tanks amounted to about 13 per cent of German tank strength. Although a small fraction of overall German tank strength, they accounted for about half of the tanks armed with a 37mm gun. By 1940, two mechanized-cavalry divisions had been rebuilt as Panzer divisions with the PzKpfw 38(t) as their principal tank. 2. leichte Division became 7. Panzer-Division and 3. leichte Division became 8. Panzer-Division. To bring their strength up to

Panzer division standards, independent regiments equipped with the new PzKpfw 38(t) tank were added to the mechanized-cavalry divisions. This included Panzer-Regiment 25, which went to the new 7. Panzer-Division, and Panzer-Regiment 10, which went to 8. Panzer-Division. Overall PzKpfw 38(t) strength on 10 May 1940 was 91 PzKpfw 38(t) and eight PzBefWg 38(t) in 7. Panzer-Division, and 116 PzKpfw 38(t) and 15 PzBefWg 38(t) in 8. Panzer-Division. Owing to lingering shortages of the PzKpfw 38(t), both divisions were fleshed out with older PzKpfw I and PzKpfw II light tanks; their medium companies were equipped with the new PzKpfw IV tanks.

7. Panzer-Division was commanded by Generalmajor Erwin Rommel during the campaign in France. It emerged as the more famous of the two divisions equipped with the PzKpfw 38(t) in France and its history is recounted below. A total of 54 PzKpfw 38(t) tanks were written off as losses after the campaign, but in fact all but six were later rebuilt at BMM.

The PzKpfw 38(t) underwent a series of modifications, some to improve its combat qualities and some to integrate it better into German service. The PzKpfw 38(t) Ausf B was ordered in July 1939, before the start of the war, and introduced German radios and German external vehicle tools. The PzKpfw 38(t) Ausf C, manufactured from May to August 1940, increased the front hull armour from 25mm to 40mm. The PzKpfw 38(t) Ausf D was essentially similar to the Ausf C except for small detail changes. The PzKpfw 38(t) Ausf E, produced

The PzBefWg 38(t) was the dedicated radio command version of the PzKpfw 38(t) fitted with a *Heckantenna* (rear antenna) for the Fu 8 transceiver. This type was used in company and higher headquarters, but also in dedicated communications as seen here with 2./PzNachAbt 83, part of the signals battalion of 7. Panzer-Division. The large 'K' on the lower bow plate is the insignia of Panzergruppe *Kleist* – XXII. Armeekorps (mot.) – at the time of the Battle of France; a command pennant is painted on the plate over the hull machine-gun station. (John Prigent)

from November 1940 to May 1941, featured improved armour. The turret front was thickened by adding a 25mm face-hardened plate over the existing 25mm plate, providing a total of 50mm of protection. Turret side armour was increased to 30mm. The upper hull sides received an additional 15mm of armour. The upper front hull on previous production tanks had been curved, but to rationalize the design for the armour increase, this plate was changed to a simple flat plate. To accommodate the extra tonne of weight, an additional leaf spring was added to the suspension. A revised rear exhaust muffler was introduced with a smoke-grenade rack in an armoured cover. The next series of PzKpfw 38(t) Ausf F was essentially similar to the Ausf E with very minor production differences. In March 1940, Sweden had ordered 90 tanks from BMM but on 18 July 1940, the OKH diverted them to the Panzer divisions as the PzKpfw 38(t) Ausf S.

The PzKpfw 38(t) again saw combat in Operation *Marita*, the invasion of Yugoslavia starting on 6 April 1941, serving again with 8. Panzer-Division. At the time of the start of Operation *Barbarossa* on 22 June 1941, the PzKpfw 38(t) equipped five of the 17 Panzer divisions taking part in the invasion of the Soviet Union. As in France, they were deployed in place of the PzKpfw III. The PzKpfw 38(t) represented about 20 per cent of the tanks taking part in the attack.

BT-7

The BT-7 was a version of the American-designed Christie tanks built under licence in the Soviet Union. Although originally based on the imported Christie M1930 convertible tank, the Soviet versions quickly departed from the American originals, particularly in terms of armament.

J. Walter Christie had begun designing self-propelled artillery for the US Army in World War I, and built his first tank shortly after the war. Early tanks were prone to mechanical breakdown during prolonged travel so a fleet of trucks was needed to transport them any long distances. To avoid this added expense, Christie designed a 'convertible' suspension system that used wheels for long-distance travel, and added tracks for cross-country travel. His first convertible tank, the M1919, was so troublesome and poorly designed that it only lasted a few months in US Army trials before Christie asked to withdraw the design for serious reworking. It returned to Army tests as the turretless M1921 but it was still badly underpowered and suffered from poor cross-country performance. It was rejected by the US Army as unsuitable. Christie then fundamentally redesigned his convertible suspension to improve the ride and to make it easier to employ. The new suspension, patented in April 1928, used identical large road-wheels on all stations except the idler and drive sprocket. When the track was removed, the last road-wheel station was powered by a chain drive off the drive sprocket while the front road-wheel steered the vehicle. The suspension used large helical springs, mounted in protected tunnels within the armoured hull, to provide a particularly smooth ride compared to that offered by the leaf-spring suspensions that predominated in international tank design at this time. The new suspension debuted on Christie's M1928 convertible tank.

The BT-5 introduced the 45mm 20K tank gun as its main armament. This is the standard 'integrated' turret developed by the Izhorsk steel works that was also used on the T-26 tank. This particular tank was knocked out in the fighting near Prokkoila, Finland on 26 August 1941. (SA-kuva)

In 1929, the Red Army created a special tank commission to tour European and American arms manufacturers to purchase modern tank designs. Although the Soviet industry was already working on new tank designs of its own, it was widely recognized that they lagged behind European and American designs. Purchase of licensed-production rights for foreign tank designs was a quick and inexpensive method by which to speed up the mechanization of the Red Army. The Soviet team originally planned to buy 50 of the new T1E2 light tanks, but after watching an impressive display of Christie's M1928, they cancelled any plans for the T1E2 and turned their attention to the Christie tank. On 28 April 1930, Christie signed a contract to provide two to the Soviet Union along with associated patent and licensed-production rights.

Christie was obliged to secure formal US government export licences for any weapons sold overseas but instead, he labelled the two tanks as 'commercial tractors' when they departed the United States on 24 December 1930. US officials were aggravated by Christie's duplicity and Soviet officials were equally annoyed when they discovered that the two 'tanks' lacked turrets or weapons. Christie had taken the easy way out by avoiding the delays and complexities of export licence. The other reasons why the tanks lacked turrets were that Christie had not designed a turret for his M1930 tank, he was already behind schedule on the delivery, and he had no access to tank guns short of obtaining them from the US Army. The turret and armament used on the Christie tanks supplied to the US Army in 1931 were designed by Rock Island Arsenal in Illinois. As a result, the Soviet government forced Christie to forfeit $25,000 for the breach of contract.

The Christie tank was accepted for Soviet production on 23 May 1931 in spite of the fact that the automotive trials had revealed numerous problems with the design. The Red Army designated the Soviet version as BT-2 and production of the new tank was assigned to the Kharkov Komintern Locomotive Plant (KhPZ) in Kharkov (now

Kharkiv, Ukraine). A simple cylindrical turret with a 37mm gun was designed for the BT-2. The hope was to complete 50 BT-2 tanks in 1931, but only three were finished in November 1931, using mild-steel plate and lacking weapons. There were substantial problems in the manufacturing process. The Kharkov plant had difficulty manufacturing Christie's large road-wheels. Production of steel armour plate proved to be a major manufacturing bottleneck. The BT-2 was powered both by reconditioned Liberty engines obtained in the United States and the Soviet copy of the Liberty, the M-5 engine. The Christie power-train was not well designed and the Liberty engine was too powerful for the transmission. As the US Army found out with their seven Christie tanks, the clutch-and-brake steering was poorly matched to such a powerful engine. The US Army rectified this problem by switching to controlled differential steering on later designs such as the T4 convertible tank, but the Soviet design team stuck with Christie's less efficient design. The BT-2 was not popular in Red Army service due to its technical immaturity, poor manufacturing quality and frequent mechanical breakdowns. Many Red Army officers regarded the 620 BT-2 tanks that were built as good for nothing other than training.

By 1932, a variety of programmes were under way at the Kharkov plant to improve the basic BT design. The Red Army had purchased licensed-production rights for the German Rheinmetall 37mm anti-tank gun. Since the infantry wanted to use it both as an infantry gun capable of firing a useful high-explosive round, as well as an anti-tank gun, the calibre was increased from 37mm to 45mm. This resulted in the 45mm 19K Model 1932 towed anti-tank gun. This gun was adapted for tank use as the 20K

The BT-7 Model 1937 introduced a new turret with the side armour angled by 15 degrees. This particular example was knocked out near Onkamus, Finland on 2 September 1941 and is being examined by Finnish officers. (SA-kuva)

A few of the early-production BT-7 Model 1937 still used the bulky 'poruchnevoy' frame antenna for the 71-TK-2 tank radio. This is evident from mountings around the turret of this tank, knocked out in the summer 1941 fighting. The wooden arms suspending the frame antenna have burned away, and the metal antenna can be seen collapsed on the hull.

and selected as the future weapon for Soviet light tanks. At the time, the Red Army was acquiring two types of light tanks, the BT for mechanizing the cavalry and the T-26, a licence-built version of the Vickers-Armstrong 6-ton tank, for infantry mechanization. To foster commonality, a standard turret was developed for both the new BT-5 tank and the T-26 using the new 45mm 20K gun and a coaxial 7.62mm DT machine gun. In 1933, the first batches of BT-5 tanks were sent to the Red Army's premier tank unit, the newly expanded 5th Kalinovskiy Mechanized Corps. In total, 1,946 BT-5 tanks were manufactured in 1933–34.

One of the main problems affecting manufacture of the BT-5 was the shortage of M-5 and reconditioned Liberty engines. A Soviet derivative of the German BMW VI aircraft engine entered production for aircraft applications as the M-17 and a tank version, down-rated from 500hp to 400hp, entered production in 1936 as the M-17T (T= *tankoviy*, tank). This was selected as the basis for the next BT variant, the BT-7. The new version also incorporated an all-welded hull, complete conversion to metric measurements, and range extension via an extended fuel tank in the rear of the hull.

One potential BT tank improvement would have been to widen the hull, the original Christie design having had an unusually narrow hull due to Christie's lack of interest in turret and armament design. The US Army had quickly moved to a wider hull on all of its follow-on designs to the Christie such as the T3E2 convertible tank and T4 medium tank. Likewise, the British adopted a wider hull design on their cruiser tanks based on the Christie tank. The wider hull not only offered more space for the crew, it also opened up the potential for more powerful armament made possible by a wider turret ring. This feature was not seriously considered by the Soviet designers until later in the decade, at which time it became an important element in the eventual T-34 design.

The Red Army placed the first production orders for the BT-7 in November 1934. The plan also incorporated a new turret design suitable for either a 45mm tank gun

BT-7 MODEL 1937, 5th TANK DIVISION

Crew: 3
Weight: 13.8 tonnes
Length: 5.66m
Width: 2.23m
Height: 2.42m
Main gun: 45mm 20K
Main gun ammunition (line/radio): 188/146
Secondary armament: Two 7.62mm DT
Machine-gun ammunition (line/radio): 2,394/1,953
Radio: 71-TK-3 (on 44% of tanks)
Hull front armour: 22mm

Hull side armour: 13mm
Turret front armour: 15mm
Max road speed (track/wheel): 52/72km/h
Cross-country speed (track): 32km/h
Road range (track/wheel): 375/500km
Terrain range (track): 160km
Fuel capacity: 650 internal +128 external litres
Engine type: M-17T
Transmission: Chain drive
Horsepower: 400

5.66m

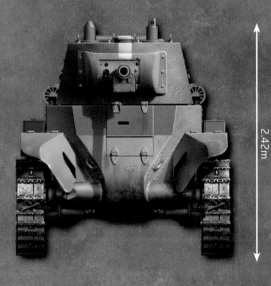

2.42m

2.23m

The BT-7 was the most widely produced version of the BT series, accounting for over 5,550 of the 8,120 manufactured. This BT-7 Model 1937 has come to grief against a tree in the Repola–Porajärvi area during the fighting near the Finnish border during late July 1941. (SA-kuva)

or a short 76mm support gun. However, the turret proved unacceptable. So as not to delay BT-7 production, the same turret used on the BT-5 was accepted as an expedient until a new turret was ready for production. The BT-7 went into large-scale production in 1935.

In April–May 1936, the Red Army tank units using the new BT-7 reported considerable technical problems, especially with the transmission which proved unable to cope with the higher power output of the new M-17T engine. As a result, the Red Army representatives at the Kharkov plant refused to accept any more BT-7 tanks until the problems were rectified. These problems came at a particularly inopportune time

A proportion of the BT-7 production was fitted with the P-40 anti-aircraft machine-gun mount, visible on this tank over the right-side loader's hatch. This particular tank, from the 5th Tank Division, is pictured near Alytus in June 1941. It is painted on the roof with the characteristic white roof cross from the occupation of the Baltic States in 1940. Judging from the open engine hatch and dismounted tow chain, it was probably abandoned after attempts to recover it had failed.

There were a variety of accessories fitted to some but not all BT-7 Model 1937 tanks. The tank nearest the camera is fitted with the twin 'combat lights', namely a pair of searchlights above the main gun intended to provide a night-fighting capability. This photograph was taken before the war during one of the parades through Palace Square in Leningrad.

as the Soviet tank industry was in the midst of a paranoid Stalinist witch-hunt for 'saboteurs'. The head of the Kharkov tank-design bureau, Afanasiy O. Firsov, was arrested and shot in 1937.

The political witch-hunt in Kharkov delayed work on BT-7 improvements. A new turret design, with the armour angled at 15 degrees, was built in early 1937 and entered production in September 1937. Other improvements adopted in 1937 included a new track with the pitch reduced to 167mm to reduce the frequency of track-shedding. The original tracks were based on the Christie design and had a nominal endurance of 2,000km, though in practice they seldom lasted more than 700–800km. They also had a tendency to shed all too easily. The new narrow-pitch tracks were also warrantied to last 2,000km, which proved optimistic. However, they extended the durability to about 1,200km on average and were also less prone to shed.

The later production batches of the BT-7 had their frontal hull armour increased from 17mm to 22mm. The original plan was to use the M-17T engine only as an interim solution pending the final development of the BD-2 diesel engine. Its 1938 production variant was redesignated as the V-2. The internal bureau designation for the BT-7 with V-2 diesel engine was A-8. Plans to switch from the BT-7 to the new diesel-engined tank were delayed by the poor durability of the early V-2 engines – seldom better than 50 operating hours instead of the objective of 200 hours. Only a few diesel-powered tanks were manufactured in 1938–39, and they were variously called the BT-7M or BT-8. Series production did not begin in earnest until 1940 and was short-lived since the Kharkov plant was switching to the manufacture of the new T-34 tank. The BT-7 was the most numerous version of the BT family, with 5,555 manufactured from 1935 to 1940.

In October 1937, work began on the BT-20, a substantially reconfigured version of the BT series with a wider hull and a BD-2 diesel engine. It eventually evolved into the A-20, A-32 and A-34, and was accepted for production at Kharkov in 1940 as the T-34 tank.

TECHNICAL
SPECIFICATIONS

CREW

The BT-7 had a crew of three: a mechanic/driver (*mekhanik-voditel*) in the front of the hull, the loader (*zaryadayushchiy*) on the right side of the turret and the commander/ gunner (*komandir/navodchik*) on the left side of the turret.

The PzKpfw 38(t) crew had one more man than the BT-7: a tank commander/ gunner (*Kommandant/Richtkanonier*) in the left side of the turret, the loader (*Ladekanonier*) in the right side of the turret, a radio operator (*Funker*) on the left side of the hull front and the driver (*Fahrer*) on the left side. The two-man turret crew was smaller than the three-man crew preferred in German medium tanks, with the commander having to double up as gunner. In this respect, the configuration was closer to that of the PzKpfw II light tank than the PzKpfw III medium tank. Unlike early German light tanks, the PzKpfw 38(t) had a vision cupola for the commander with protected episcopes. The fighting compartment was very cramped and did not provide adequate room for normal crew stowage. As will be noted in the photographs of tanks of 7. Panzer-Division, most PzKpfw 38(t) had additional expedient stowage bins fitted externally.

In terms of situational awareness, the PzKpfw 38(t) had a significant advantage in the provision of a cupola for the commander which permitted relatively easy vision all around the tank. In addition, the commander's hatch was designed to open to the right rear, enabling him to operate with his head outside the tank. The

The crew layout of the PzKpfw 38(t) was conventional, with the commander/gunner in the left side of the turret under the cupola, the loader to the left of the gun, the bow gunner/radio operator in the left hull front, and the driver in the right hull front.

BT-7 commander had a periscopic sight for external vision, but this was awkward to use compared to a cupola. In addition, the hatches on the BT-7 opened forward and locked in a near-vertical position, blocking the forward view and preventing the commander from observing the terrain forward. Soviet tank tactics preferred the commander to remain under armour, while German tactics preferred that a commander operate with his head outside the tank whenever possible for better situational awareness in spite of the greater risk of being wounded.

Although the BT-7 was significantly larger than the PzKpfw 38(t), there were fewer crewmen. This was in large measure due to the narrow hull, especially in the forward portion of the tank.

The turret interior of the BT-7 Model 1937 was not especially spacious. The commander/gunner sat on the left side of the turret while the loader sat on the right. (SA-kuva)

In terms of internal command-and control, both tanks were similar. The crewmen communicated with each other via an internal intercom system with each crewman having earphones that connected to intercom boxes on the walls; voice transmission was by throat-microphone. In terms of tank radio distribution, German tanks were not as well equipped as many historians assume, nor were the Soviet tanks as poorly supplied as has been widely claimed. Both German and Soviet tank units used flags and flare pistols as alternate methods of communicating between tanks.

Not all German tanks had a full radio transceiver (transmitter/receiver) at this time. The PzKpfw 38(t) platoon commanders received a Fu 2 receiver and Fu 5 radio transceiver set while the rest of the platoon tanks only had the Fu 2 receiver. Due to the limited space inside the PzKpfw 38(t), many platoon commanders' tanks had the hull machine gun removed to provide adequate space for the transceiver set. The Fu 5 operated in the 27.2–33.3MHz bandwidth with a 10W output and a range when stationary of 6km in telegraph mode and 4km in voice mode. German tanks had the advantage of better-quality radios that had a more robust tuner.

Slightly fewer than half (44 per cent) of BT-7 tanks were fitted with radio transceivers. Some of the initial production BT-7 still had older radio sets such as the 71-TK-2, but most were fitted with the 71-TK-3 Shakal (Jackal). The earlier versions of the Shakal family used a bulky frame antenna around the turret, but the 71-TK-3 introduced a more practical whip antenna. The radio transceiver was located in the rear turret bustle and was operated by the tank commander. The 71-TK-3 operated in the 4.0–5.625MHz bandwidth with a 3–5W output and a maximum range when stationary of 15km in voice mode and 30km in telegraph mode. The transmitter/receiver combination was quite bulky and so tanks fitted with radios carried less machine-gun ammunition in the bustle. The problem with Soviet tank radios was not the lack of distribution, but their fragility in field conditions in which it was difficult to keep them properly tuned, and a lack of trained operators.

PROTECTION

The BT-7 tank, like most designs of the early 1930s, was not especially well armoured. Hull frontal armour in the early versions was only 13mm thick, sufficient to protect against 7.62mm machine-gun fire. On the BT-7 Model 1937 production series, this was boosted to 22mm frontal armour, intended to protect against heavy machine guns. Turret armour was 15mm on both early and later BT-7 tanks, though the BT-7 Model 1937 introduced sloped armour which marginally improved effective armour thickness to about 16mm equivalent. As a result, the BT-7 could be penetrated by the 37mm gun on the PzKpfw 38(t) at any normal battle range.

Development of the PzKpfw 38(t) began later than the BT-7 and its armour was better than that of the BT-7. The early-production series had 25mm armour on the hull front and turret front from the outset. Side armour, as on the BT-7, was modest at 15mm. As a result of early combat experiences, the frontal armour was increased on Ausf E and Ausf F tanks by adding 25mm of armour to the hull and turret front, bringing it to 50mm in total, and increasing the turret side armour to 30mm. In theory, the 50mm frontal armour could be penetrated by the Soviet 45mm tank gun at ranges under 100m; in practice, this armour was sufficient to protect the PzKpfw 38(t) frontally against the Soviet 45mm tank gun.

PzKpfw 38(t) crews complained that its riveted armour plate worsened the effects of any penetration. Otto Carius, a PzKpfw 38(t) gunner in Panzer-Regiment 21 (20. Panzer-Division), recalled such an incident on 8 July 1941 in his classic memoir *Tigers in the Mud*:

> It happened like greased lightning. A hit against our tank, a metallic crack, the scream of a comrade, and that was all there was. A large piece of armor plating had been penetrated next to the radio operator's seat. No one had to tell us to get out. Not until I had run my hand across my face while crawling in the ditch next to the road did I discover they had also got me. Our radio operator had lost his left arm. We cursed the brittle and inelastic Czech steel that had given the Russian 45mm gun so little trouble. The pieces of our own armor plating and the assembly bolts caused considerably more damage than the shrapnel of the round itself.

Carius lost several front teeth, most likely when his face smashed into some part of the turret interior upon the impact of the Soviet projectile. Although the BT-7 used welded rather than riveted construction, its thin armour was hard and brittle, and subject to breaking off in slabs when hit by armour-piercing gun projectiles.

FIREPOWER

The PzKpfw 38(t) was armed with a 37mm Škoda A7 (L/48) gun, designated as the 3.7cm KwK 38(t) by the Germans. It was aimed by means of a Turmzielfernrohr 38(t) telescopic sight with 2.6× magnification and a 25-degree field of view. This was

PzKpfw 38(t) TURRET

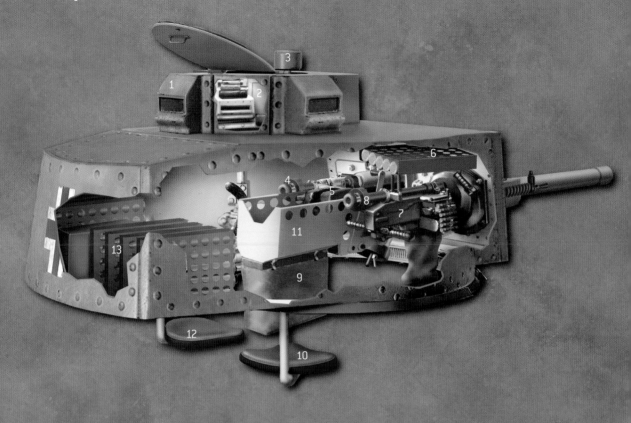

1. Commander's cupola
2. Commander's vision block
3. Commander's periscopic sight
4. Commander/gunner's telescopic sight
5. 3.7cm KwK 38(t) gun breech
6. Loader's ready ammunition rack
7. 7.92mm MG 37(t) machine gun
8. telescopic sight for machine gun
9. Shell catching bag
10. Loader's seat
11. Gun safety cage
12. Commander/gunner's seat
13. Rear bustle 3.7cm ammunition stowage
14. 3.7cm PzgrPatr 34(t) umg (armour-piercing-tracer)
15. 3.7cm SprgrPatr 34(t) (high explosive)

BT-7 TURRET

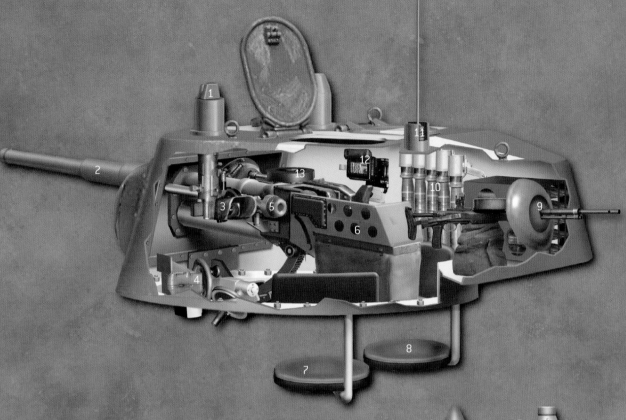

1. Gunner's periscopic sight head
2. 45mm 20K main gun
3. Commander/gunner's periscopic sight
4. Turret rotation wheel
5. Gunner's telescopic sight
6. Gun safety cage
7. Commander/gunner's seat
8. Loader's seat
9. Rear DT machine gun
10. 45mm ammunition stowage
11. Radio antenna for 71-TK-3 transceiver
12. Loader's side vision port
13. Co-axial DT machine gun
14. 45mm BR-243 (armour-piercing-tracer)
15. 45mm UO-243 (high explosive)

This illustration of the 3.7cm KwK 37 gun from the PzKpfw 38(t) manual shows the mounting from the loader's side on the left. The 7.92mm MG 37(t) machine gun could be locked coaxially with the main gun, or it could be separately aimed by the loader since it was fitted to its own ball mount.

supplemented with a Turmrundblickfernrohr 38(t) periscopic sight mounted on the roof with 2.6× magnification and a 25-degree field of view. Unlike the periscopic sight on the BT-7 tank, this sight was used for surveillance and was not mechanically linked to the gun. The gun fired a 37mm round with better anti-armour performance than the German 37mm gun: 35mm vs 29mm armour penetration at 500m. The basic round was the 3.7cm PzgrPatr 37(t) armour-piercing round which was followed by the improved 3.7cm PzgrPatr 37(t) umg which added a tracer. A third anti-tank round, the 3.7cm Pzgr 40/37(t), was introduced in March 1941; its tungsten-carbide core could penetrate 64mm of armour at 30 degrees at 100m. These rounds were very expensive to produce due to the scarcity of tungsten carbide and so were not in widespread service in June 1941. The round was issued later in 1941 due to the threat posed by the T-34 medium tank. Ammunition stowage was 90 rounds of 3.7cm.

In terms of secondary armament, the PzKpfw 38(t) was armed with two 7.92mm ZB vz. 37 machine guns, called MG 37(t) by the Germans. One of these machine guns was located on the right side of the hull front with the machine-gunner doubling as the vehicle's radio operator. The turret machine gun was in a separate ball mount and so could be employed separately from the main gun by the loader, or locked to the main gun for use as a coaxial weapon. A total of 2,700 rounds of 7.92mm machine-gun ammunition was carried.

The BT-7 was armed with the standard Soviet 45mm 20K tank gun. It was aimed using a TOP Model 1930 telescopic gun sight offering 2.5× magnification and a 15-degree field of view. The stabilized TOS sight, introduced on some later-production tanks, was gyro-stabilized in the vertical axis. The gunner was also provided with a PT1 periscopic tank sight mounted on the roof. This was mechanically linked to the gun mount and could be used as an alternative means of aiming the 45mm tank gun. Like the telescope, it had 2.5× magnification, but offered a wider field of view of 26 degrees. It could also be traversed half circle, and so was used as the commander's principal external-observation device. A second periscopic sight could be fitted on the right side of the turret for the loader, though in practice the expense of these sights meant that most tanks had only one. In terms of performance, the Soviet 45mm tank gun was similar in anti-tank performance to the Czechoslovak 37mm gun, slightly better at closer ranges, but with performance dropping off at 500m due to the greater weight and drag of the larger and heavier projectile. It had better high-explosive performance than the 3.7cm SprgrPatr(t) due to a larger high-explosive fill: 118g of TNT versus about 25g in the 37mm round.

Secondary armament on the BT-7 varied considerably. All tanks had the basic 7.62mm DT machine gun as a coaxial weapon next to the main gun. A proportion of the BT-7 production tanks were fitted with the P-40 anti-aircraft machine-gun mounting over the upper right turret opening. These tanks were sometimes designated as BT-7zen (zen = *zenitniy*: anti-aircraft). Some tanks were also fitted with a ball mounting in the rear of the turret bustle that enabled a DT machine gun to be fitted for defence against infantry close attack. Tanks without radios could carry up to 3,339 rounds of machine-gun ammunition; radio tanks carried only 2,016 rounds.

Overall, the firepower of both tanks was similar. The PzKpfw 38(t) had the advantage in tank-vs-tank combat since its main gun was more than adequate in

A portion of BT-7s were fitted with the P-40 anti-aircraft machine gun mount over the loader's hatch. This was a fitting to permit the use of the 7.62mm DT machine gun in an anti-aircraft role. This mount was also fitted to other tanks of the period, including the KV-1 as shown here.

penetrating the thin armour of the BT-7. The BT-7 had difficulties in penetrating the frontal armour of the PzKpfw 38(t) when dealing with the later models of tanks that had the thicker 50mm armour.

Comparative tank gun performance		
	PzKpfw 38(t)	**BT-7**
Gun	3.7cm KwK 38(t)	45mm 20K
Calibre	37mm	45mm
Barrel length	L/47.8	L/46
Armour-piercing round	PzgrPatr 37(t) umg	BR-240
Weight of round	0.85kg	1.43kg
Initial velocity	741m/sec	757m/sec
Armour penetration (mm) @ 100m @ 0 degrees	49mm	52mm
Armour penetration (mm) @ 100m @ 30 degrees	40.5mm	43mm
Armour penetration (mm) @ 500m @ 0 degrees	42.5mm	38mm
Armour penetration (mm) @ 500m @ 30 degrees	34.8mm	31mm

MOBILITY

The PzKpfw 38(t) was powered by a Praga Typ TNHPS/II 125hp petrol engine giving the tank a power-to-weight ratio of 12.7hp/tonne. The BT-7 had a much more powerful engine, the 400hp M-17T, giving it more than double the PzKpfw 38(t) power-to-weight ratio at 29hp/tonne. The BT-7 had a much higher road speed than the PzKpfw 38(t), 72km/h in wheeled mode. However, the horsepower advantage did not translate into greater mobility advantages in normal tracked mode, and both tanks had similar tracked road speeds of about 55km/h and similar cross-country speeds of about 30km/h. The road-wheel travel on both tanks was very similar, about 300mm, with the BT-7 offering a slightly smoother or mushier ride due to the use of vertical springs compared to the stiffer ride offered by leaf springs on the PzKpfw 38(t). The power-train arrangement on both tanks was different, with the PzKpfw 38(t) having the transmission located in the hull front while the BT-7 had it in the rear behind the engine. In general, the PzKpfw 38(t) was easier to drive due to the proximity of the driver to the transmission and the use of a more advanced Praga-Wilson transmission.

The Wehrmacht expected logistical problems in Russia and so fitted most of the tanks committed to Operation *Barbarossa* with special fuel trailers for carrying additional 200-litre fuel drums. This PzKpfw 38(t) of Panzer-Regiment 25 (7. Panzer-Division) is passing a knocked-out T-34 of the 9th Tank Regiment (5th Tank Division) during the fighting near Alytus on 22 June 1941. (NARA)

On the BT-7, control of the transmission was managed through a series of long actuating rods located on the floor of the hull. Manipulating the transmission via these rods required strength and skill, and small misalignments could make operating the control much more difficult. Inadequate driver training in the Red Army combined with the crudity of the BT-7 transmission system increased the number of mechanical breakdowns and driving accidents. A bad habit common among inexperienced drivers was to shift into second gear once moving, and then control tank speed using only the accelerator rather than trying to shift to the higher gears due to the difficulties inherent in the transmission system. This caused premature mechanical exhaustion of the engine and transmission. Neither tank type was well protected against dust intrusion, which was particularly bad on the BT-7 due to poor air and oil filtration. In addition, the magneto was not well protected against dust, which could prevent proper engine starting.

The PzKpfw 38(t) had a 220-litre internal fuel tank providing a range of about 250km on the road and 100km cross-country. In view of the distances expected to be undertaken during Operation *Barbarossa*, the Wehrmacht fitted many tanks with special fuel trailers (Anhänger für 200-Liter-Kraftstoff-Faß) that carried a single 200-litre fuel drum, essentially doubling the tank's range. These fuel trailers were not especially popular with tank crews since they made it very awkward to back up and manoeuvre, to say nothing of their vulnerability to enemy fire. They were seldom seen after the first few days of the campaign, as will be noticed in the accompanying photographs. Most PzKpfw 38(t) also had an additional rack for 5-litre jerricans. The M-17T engine on the BT-7 was a gas-guzzler and so the tank carried considerably more fuel than the PzKpfw 38(t), consisting of 650 litres in the internal tank and four trackguard-mounted cells with a further 128 litres. This gave the BT-7 a road range of about 500km on wheels and 250km on tracks; cross-country range on tracks was about 160km.

A column of PzKpfw 38(t) of Panzer-Regiment 25 heads towards Kalvarija on the morning of 22 June 1941 shortly after having crossed the German–Soviet frontier. The tank on the right is towing one of the special fuel trailers adopted for Operation *Barbarossa*. (NARA)

33

THE COMBATANTS

7. PANZER-DIVISION

The early roots of the Panzer divisions up to the Battle of France in 1940 have been covered in previous Duel titles, so the description here is abbreviated.[1] The German unit at the centre of this Duel is Panzer-Regiment 25, the tank element of 7. Panzer-Division in 1941. This regiment was formed on 12 October 1937 in Erlangen, in Wehrkreis XIII (Military District 13) in Franconia, based around a cadre of two companies from Panzer-Regiment 3. At the time of the Polish campaign in 1939, it was only partially formed with a single incomplete battalion and it did not see combat. One of the lessons of the Polish campaign was that the mechanized-cavalry division (*leichte Division*) was not as combat-effective as the Panzer division. As a result, the mechanized-cavalry divisions were reorganized into Panzer divisions, and the partially formed Panzer-Regiment 25 became part of this process when it was assigned to 2. leichte Division during its conversion to 7. Panzer-Division. The division came under command of Generalmajor Erwin Rommel in February 1940.

As part of the reorganization, I./PzRgt 25 was re-equipped with the PzKpfw 38(t) starting in February 1940, replacing most of its old light tanks though some PzKpfw II remained. Panzer-Regiment 25 was substantially reinforced in late 1939, and its second battalion was created in April 1940 using the three tank companies of I./PzRgt 23. At the time of the French campaign, Panzer-Regiment 25 had a truncated, two-battalion organization. 7. Panzer-Division incorporated the original tank formation of 2. leichte

---

1   See Steven J. Zaloga, *Panzer IV vs Char B1 bis: France 1940*, Duel 33 (2011), and *Panzer III vs Somua S 35: Belgium 1940*, Duel 63 (2014), both published by Osprey.

Division, Panzer-Abteilung 66, which was re-equipped with PzKpfw 38(t) starting in March 1940. This unit was sometimes referred to as III./PzRgt 25 though in fact it was not officially incorporated into the regiment until February 1941.

7. Panzer-Division was one of two Panzer divisions that were equipped with the PzKpfw 38(t) during the campaign in France, the other being 8. Panzer-Division. 7. Panzer-Division was dubbed the 'Ghost Division' (*Gespensterdivision*) after its exploits in France. The division served with 4. Armee, part of Heeresgruppe A which executed the 'sickle cut' through the Ardennes. It was not part of the armoured spearhead of Panzergruppe *Kleist*, but served on its right flank.

The PzKpfw 38(t) proved well suited to Rommel's tactics. Instead of directly confronting the French armoured force, Rommel exploited his division's mobility by using a modern version of the classic infiltration tactics of 1918. Having penetrated the Belgian border defences, Rommel's tanks pushed down the Morville–Flavion road towards an inevitable confrontation with the French 1re division cuirassée. The French armoured divisions were substantially smaller than their German opponents, but they were equipped with the powerful Char B1 bis heavy tank and the well-armoured Hotchkiss H 39 infantry tank. Oberst Karl Rothenburg's Panzer-Regiment 25 was confronted by a Char B1 bis company of the 28e bataillon de chars de combat (BCC: tank battalion) outside Flavion. Five German tanks were hit in quick succession. Rommel's eye was not on a pitched tank battle, and so he dispatched his divisional Flak batteries with 8.8cm guns to keep the Char B1 bis tanks at bay while his division continued westwards. During the advance later in the morning, Rommel's forces caught the rest of the 28e BCC (Char B1 bis) and 25e BCC (H 39) when they were vulnerable during refuelling, disrupted them, but kept moving forward. He left it up to the neighbouring 5. Panzer-Division to deal with the remaining threat of the 1re division cuirassée.

By 19 May 1940, 7. Panzer-Division was in the vanguard of 4. Armee and reached the Cambrai area. This placed it in the middle of the tank battles around Arras against French and British units during the second week of the campaign. Once again, Rommel refrained from pitting his thinly armoured PzKpfw 38(t) tanks against the thickly armoured Allied tanks, and the division's infantry and 8.8cm guns bore the brunt of the Allied tank attacks. 7. Panzer-Division remained on the western side of the Dunkirk pocket until early June 1940. The PzKpfw 38(t) proved well suited to a campaign of rapid movement, but it was not ideal for tank-vs-tank fighting. Its 37mm gun was poorly suited to fighting against the thickly armoured French tanks, which were nearly impervious from the front. Rommel's tactics made best use of the PzKpfw 38(t)'s mobility while minimizing its inadequate firepower and armour when dealing with the French tanks. The successes of the 'Ghost Division' were won more often by boldness and mobility than either firepower or armoured protection.

Officers of Panzer-Regiment 25 consult with 7. Panzer-Division commander Generalmajor Hans Freiherr von Funck during the fighting to contain the Minsk pocket on 29 June 1941. (NARA)

Following the evacuation of the British Expeditionary Force from Dunkirk, 7. Panzer-Division took part in the push southwards past Rouen, again spearheading 4. Armee and executing the breakthrough to the Seine River. It reached Fécamp on the Channel coast on 10 June. During the third week of June, it took part in the push through Lower Normandy, eventually taking part in the capture of Cherbourg on 20 June. Its exemplary performance came at a price, however, as the division suffered higher troop casualties in France than any other Panzer division. Its vehicle losses included 42 tanks of which 26 were PzKpfw 38(t). It claimed about 460 French tanks and armoured cars destroyed or captured, and took more than 97,000 Allied prisoners.

The campaign in France in 1940 provided 7. Panzer-Division with invaluable combat experience. It remained in France after the campaign and initially was assigned to the Operation *Seelöwe* plan for the invasion of Great Britain. When Rommel was ordered to North Africa in February 1941 to lead German forces there, divisional command went to Generalmajor Hans Freiherr von Funck. He had commanded the German military units in Spain during the Spanish Civil War of 1936–39, and had led Panzer-Brigade 3 of 3. Panzer-Division during the campaign in France. The division left France in February 1941 and was temporarily stationed in the Bonn–Bad Godesberg area of Germany before being sent to East Prussia in the summer of 1941 for the planned invasion of the Soviet Union. At the start of Operation *Barbarossa* on 22 June 1941, 7. Panzer-Division had a total of 53 PzKpfw II, 167 PzKpfw 38(t), seven PzBefWg 38(t), 30 PzKpfw IV and eight PzBefWg III.

7. Panzer-Division (Generalmajor Hans Freiherr von Funck)

Panzer-Regiment 25 (Oberst Karl Rothenburg)

    I. Abteilung (Major Schulz)
    II. Abteilung (Major Dr Schirmer)
    III. Abteilung (Oberstleutnant Thomale)

Schützen-Brigade 7 (Oberst Hans Freiherr von Boineburg-Lengsfeld)

Schützen-Regiment 6 (Oberst Erich von Unger)

    I. Bataillon (Major Stroebe)
    II. Bataillon (Major Junck)

Schützen-Regiment 7 (Oberst Carl-Hans Lungershausen)

    I. Bataillon (Major Hansen)
    II. Bataillon (Oberstleutnant Hasso von Manteuffel)

Kradschützen-Bataillon 7 (Major von Steinkeller)

Artillerie-Regiment 78 (Oberst Gottfried Frölich)

    I. Abteilung (Hauptmann Oll)
    II. Abteilung (Hauptmann Schwarz)
    III. Abteilung (Major von Kronhelm)

Panzer-Aufklärungs-Abteilung 37 (Major Freiherr von Paar zu Schönau von Riederer)

Panzerjäger-Abteilung 42 (Major Witt)

Panzer-Pionier-Bataillon 58 (Oberstleutnant von Mertens)

Nachrichten-Abteilung 83 (Major Müller)

KARL ROTHENBURG

Karl Rothenburg was born at Fürstenwalde on 8 June 1894. Aged 19, he joined 3. Kompanie, 5. Garde-Regiment zu Fuß (5th Guards Foot Regiment) on 1 April 1914. He took part in the battle of Namur in Belgium before the regiment went to the Eastern Front, fighting around the Masurian Lakes and then in southern Poland. He was promoted to *Unteroffizier* on 21 December 1914. During 1914, he was awarded the Iron Cross 1st and 2nd Class as well as the Wound Badge. The regiment returned to the Western Front in the autumn of 1915 and he was promoted to *Leutnant der Reserve* on 18 November 1915. In 1916, he was acting commander of 2. Kompanie which fought on the Somme, and he became permanent commander of the company in April 1917. Rothenburg's unit took part in the March offensive of 1918 in the breakthrough between Gouzeaucourt and Vermand, and he was wounded again on 29 March. He was awarded the Knight's Cross of the Hohenzollern House Order with Swords on 23 May 1918 for his leadership during the offensive and the Pour le Mérite (Blue Max) on 30 June 1918 for leading his company in the capture of the Ricquebourg Wood and the crossing of the Matz brook.

Oberst Karl Rothenburg.

Rothenburg left the Army at the end of 1918 and joined the Schutzpolizei in Thüringia in 1924. He served as an officer in Jena, as a major and police commander in Weimar in 1930 and as an *Oberstleutnant* at Sondershausen in 1934. He returned to the Army with a *Major*'s rank on 26 July 1935, became commander of II./PzRgt 6 on 1 August 1936, and regimental commander on 1 March 1939. The regiment served in the 1939 campaign in Poland where Rothenburg was again decorated with the Iron Cross 1st and 2nd Class. He took command of Panzer-Regiment 25 in February 1940 and was decorated with the Knight's Cross on 3 June 1940 for his leadership during the campaign in France. During the initial fighting in the Soviet Union, Rothenburg was wounded on 28 June near Minsk when a damaged Soviet armoured train exploded. Although offered transport by a Fieseler Storch aircraft or armoured car, Rothenburg instead took a staff car back to the rear. The car was ambushed and Rothenburg killed. He was a popular commander and Panzer-Regiment 25 was nicknamed Panzer-Regiment Rothenburg afterwards. He was posthumously promoted to *Generalmajor*.

THE 5th TANK DIVISION

The Red Army's mechanized forces underwent a series of disruptions in 1936–41 that left them in a constant state of turmoil. The Red Army formed its first four mechanized corps in 1932–34, each consisting of a T-26 tank brigade, a BT tank brigade and an infantry brigade with a total of 430 tanks and 215 armoured cars each. The new BT tanks were also used in the new independent mechanized brigades and in mechanized regiments attached to the horsed-cavalry divisions.

The purges which tortured Soviet Russia from 1936 to 1941 are among the most grotesque passages in modern European history. In 1936, Stalin began to stifle any possible political opposition in a series of show trials and executions. In June 1937, he turned his malignant attention to the Army. The Red Army lost three of five Marshals, 14 of 16 Army commanders, 60 of 67 corps commanders, 136 of 199 divisional commanders, 221 of 397 brigade commanders, and thousands of lower-ranking officers. The new mechanized formations were particularly hard hit due to their association with Marshal Mikhail Tukhachevskiy, the main proponent of mechanized deep operations. Many tank experts and designers were killed including General Innokentiy A. Khalepskiy and Afanasiy O. Firsov. Through the mid-1930s, the Red Army had been chronically unable to train enough officers, especially for the mechanized force, and the purges made the situation much worse.

In 1938, the Red Army's tank units underwent another reorganization. The four mechanized corps were reorganized as tank corps with 600 tanks and 12,710 troops. The majority of the Army's tanks belonged to 25 independent tank brigades (four heavy and 21 light tank brigades), the BT mechanized regiments in the cavalry divisions, and a large number T-26 battalions in the rifle divisions. A small number of Soviet tank troops took part in the Spanish Civil War on the side of the Republic. The lessons of the Spanish Civil War proved largely irrelevant to Red Army tactical doctrine as the purges had terrorized most thoughtful observers into silence, and the conservative cronies of Stalin were happy to distort the Spanish experiences to fit their own dubious preconceptions.

On 17 September 1939, the Soviet Union invaded eastern Poland in keeping with the secret Molotov–Ribbentrop Pact with Nazi Germany. Among the invading units were the 15th and 25th Tank corps as well as scores of tank battalions and cavalry tank brigades. The Soviet thrusts were not met with any significant resistance since the Poles were already preoccupied with the Germans. In the wake of the Polish campaign, the Red Army tank corps were disbanded. In their place came four shrunken motorized divisions with about 275 tanks apiece, about half the strength in tanks of the previous corps. The Red Army continued in this retrograde direction, turning away from Tukhachevskiy's deep battle ideas in favour of a closer subordination of the tank units to the infantry and cavalry. In November 1939, the Red Army invaded Finland, expecting a quick victory. Instead, the Finns fought the Soviets to a bloody standstill that lasted more than three months, and cost the Red Army about 350,000 casualties. Tank losses totalled 3,200 tanks of all types of which 1,920 were combat losses and 1,275 were the result of mechanical breakdowns and accidents. The Finnish campaign was humiliating evidence of the disarray of the Red Army, the consequence of the slaughter of the Army's professional officers. The poor performance of the Red Army in Finland convinced Hitler that the Soviet Union was no more than a paper tiger, which reinforced his inclination to attack his erstwhile ally.

The next blow came in May and June 1940, when the Germans swept through the Low Countries and France. The astonishing defeat of the highly regarded French Army at the hands of the German Panzer force made it clear, even to Stalin, that the disbandment of the tank corps had been a fundamental mistake. In June 1940, the Red Army made another wild change of course, initially forming nine massive mechanized corps along with plans to add a further 21 starting in March 1941. The 1940 mechanized corps was a true corps in the Western sense of the word, being composed of two tank divisions, a motorized division and corps troops including an HQ and staff, a motorcycle regiment, communications and engineer battalions and an aircraft cooperation squadron. Each tank division had two tank regiments, a moto-rifle regiment and an artillery regiment, and totalled 375 tanks and 11,343 men. The official table of equipment called for 210 T-34 medium tanks, 63 KV heavy tanks and 102 T-26 or BT tanks per division, though the new types were not available in sufficient numbers in 1941 to meet this objective.

The enormity of these new formations underscored the acute shortage of trained mechanized unit commanders. Only the fielding of a small number of gargantuan formations could prevent the limited pool of even marginally competent officers from being totally exhausted. The corps tables, however, called for 31,574 tanks while fewer than 24,000 were available, so they could not be fully equipped until 1942 at the earliest; Stalin had expected the Franco-German conflict to last for years. What made the situation worse was that 29 per cent of the existing Soviet tanks required major factory overhaul and 44 per cent required rebuilding in district workshops. In other words, only 27 per cent or about 7,000 tanks were in good enough mechanical condition to last more than a few days of fighting before suffering mechanical breakdown.

To add further to the disruption, the Soviet absorption of eastern Poland and the Baltic States in 1939–40 forced the Red Army to deploy many of its premier tank units forward to old Tsarist military garrisons in the western borderlands which lacked the modern facilities needed to maintain and supply mechanized formations. These bases lacked repair facilities, tank gunnery ranges, fuel depots and other facilities essential to daily tank training and maintenance.

The Red Army's 5th Tank Division, the centrepiece of this study, provides a microcosm of the trials and tribulations of the Red Army in the years before the German invasion. The core of the division was the 2nd Light Tank Brigade. In 1939, this brigade was part of the 15th Tank Corps of the Belorussian Military District. The brigade was commanded by Aleksei V. Kurkin who had a long career in the Soviet armoured force, first having commanded an armoured train in the Russian Civil War. He was young enough and junior enough to have escaped the purges, and was appointed to command the 2nd

Major Stepan I. Aksenov's 1st Tank Battalion, 9th Tank Regiment was equipped with T-28 medium tanks that had formerly belonged to the 21st Heavy Tank Brigade. They were in poor mechanical shape in 1941 and many were abandoned after they broke down. This one took part in the attempts to repel the attacks by Panzer-Regiment 25 on the east side of the Alytus town bridge on 22 June. (NARA)

Light Tank Brigade in April 1938. The brigade was mostly equipped with the new BT-7 Model 1937 and took part in the invasion of Poland starting on 17 September 1939. The 15th Tank Corps crossed the Polish frontier south of Minsk and headed for Grodno (now Grodna, Belarus) at the junction of East Prussia and Lithuania. The brigade reached Sokółka, south-west of Grodno, by 20 September, by which time it had lost four BT-7 tanks in combat and 13 broken down out of its original 240 tanks during its 300km road-march.

In the wake of the Polish campaign, the Soviet Union gradually absorbed the Baltic States as part of the Molotov–Ribbentrop Pact. Three special rifle corps were formed for this purpose: the 65th Special Rifle Corps (*Osobovoe-Strelkoviy Korpus*) for Estonia, the 2nd Special Rifle Corps for Latvia and the 16th Special Rifle Corps for Lithuania. On 24 September 1939, the Soviet government gave Estonia an ultimatum, insisting that the country sign a mutual assistance pact and agree to the permanent stationing of Soviet troops in the country. This was followed on 5 and 10 October 1939 with similar ultimatums to Latvia and Lithuania. After the German attack on the Low Countries in 1940, Moscow decided to incorporate the Baltic States directly into the Soviet Union. It issued new ultimatums on 15–16 June 1940, followed by occupation of the countries by the three corps. The plans included the disarming of the Baltic States' armies, so a more heavily armed contingent was involved. In the case of Lithuania, the 16th Special Rifle Corps was reinforced by Kurkin's 2nd Light Tank Brigade, which amounted to about 240 of the 310 tanks involved in the uncontested occupation of the country. This involved another 300km road-march, which further wore down the brigade's BT-7 tanks.

Lithuania had been a part of the Russian Empire prior to 1918, so in most cases the Red Army took over former Tsarist Army bases. In the case of the 2nd Light Tank Brigade, it was deployed to the garrison town of Alytus on the Neman River near the border with East Prussia. There were two old fortified military camps south of the town, with most of the brigade located in the larger southern base that guarded the bridge over the Neman River at Kaniūkai.

The new 3rd Mechanized Corps was formed in Lithuania in June 1940 using the headquarters and staff of the 24th Rifle Corps. The new 5th Tank Division was formed around Kurkin's 2nd Light Tank Brigade, reinforced with T-28 tanks of the 21st Heavy Tank Brigade from Minsk and the tank battalion of the 121st Rifle Division. The corps' new 2nd Tank Division was formed in Vilnius from the 7th Cavalry Division's tank regiment plus two tank regiments from the 21st Heavy Tank Brigade. The 84th Moto-Rifle Division was reorganized in Yanov (Yaniv, Ukraine) from the 84th Rifle Division, reinforced with the tank battalions of three rifle divisions.

Aleksei Kurkin was appointed to command the new 5th Tank Division; its headquarters and staff were largely those of the previous 2nd Light Tank Brigade at Alytus. His assistant commander was Pavel Rotmistrov who had commanded a tank brigade in Finland and who would become famous as the commander of the 5th Guards Tank Army at Kursk in 1943. The division expanded its footprint, taking over the northern garrison in Alytus where its howitzer regiment, air-defence battalion and pontoon-bridge battalion were stationed. The Alytus garrison lacked suitable ranges to practise tank driving or tank gunnery and so the troops had to travel about 40km for practice at the Lithuanian Army ranges near the air base at Varėna. The Alytus

FËDOR F. FËDOROV

Fëdor Fëdorov was born in Odessa, Ukraine on 25 January 1900. He joined the Red Army in 1918, serving first in the Filippov Brigade and then on the staff of the 45th Brigade. In 1924 he became a cadet in the Mechanization School of the Leningrad Military District and after graduation he was assigned to lead a platoon of the 1st Automotive Battalion of the Moscow Military District. In March 1933, he became a battalion commander at the Moscow School of Tank Specialists. In February 1935 he was appointed a tank-battalion commander in the 2nd Rifle Division in the Caucasus, and a year later the commander of the 14th Mechanized Regiment of the 12th Cavalry Division. He served as a military adviser in Spain to the Republican tank units during the Spanish Civil War of 1936–39. On his return to the Soviet Union he was placed under investigation by the NKVD secret police due to suspicions that he had visited his wife's exiled brothers, Princes Alexei and Vasily Urusov, in France; charges were never filed and he escaped imprisonment.

On 11 December 1938, Fëdorov was promoted to colonel and took command of a tank regiment. He took a tank-officer refresher course and was initially appointed to a staff position in the new 3rd Mechanized Corps. He was subsequently transferred to lead the new 5th Tank Division on 25 April 1941 when General Aleksei V. Kurkin was elevated to corps command. Fëdorov was wounded on 18 July 1941 while in command of the remnants of the 5th Tank Division. On 20 August 1941, he was appointed chief of the Tank-Automotive Centre in Moscow. During the defence of Moscow, he led an improvised armoured unit at the front. Biographical details after the Moscow campaign are sketchy, mentioning only that he took part in the fighting at Stalingrad and Leningrad but with no detail of his positions, and he does not appear to have been awarded any major decorations. Towards the end of the war, he led the Solikamsk tank school. He subsequently contracted typhus and died on 20 January 1945.

Colonel Fëdor F. Fëdorov.

garrison had no tank hangars for storage or maintenance and so the tanks were maintained and stored outside.

The division's tanks were not in the best of condition due to their use in the invasion of Poland and the subsequent occupation of Lithuania. The T-28s had served in the 21st Heavy Tank Brigade in Poland in 1939, and were worn out. Of the 57 T-28s in the 3rd Mechanized Corps, only 24 were serviceable; 29 required depot overhaul and four were non-functional and required factory reconstruction. Detailed data on the division's BT-7 tank fleet is not available. However, the BT-7 required a medium rebuilding at district depots after 200 engine hours and a factory rebuild at 600 hours. Tracks had to be replaced every 2,000km, though in practice it was closer to 1,200km. Owing to their use in 1939–40, many of the tanks would have been on the waiting list for such work. This was complicated by the fact that the 5th Tank Division was now forward-deployed in the new Baltic Special Military District (*Pribaltitskoe osobovoe voennoe okrug*) which lacked the usual district infrastructure. Another problem was that there was a significant shortage of spare parts for the BT-7 due to a decision in 1940–41 to switch priority to the construction of the new T-34 tank at the Kharkov plant. Barely 20 per cent of the needed parts were funded in 1941.

The way around this problem was to retire the most worn-out BT tanks as the new T-34 became available. As a result, the number of BT tanks in the division fell from 258 on 20 October 1940 to 170 on the eve of war, while 50 new T-34 tanks were sent to replace them. Of these new T-34 tanks, the 30 delivered on 4 February 1941 were the T-34 Model 1940 with the original 76mm L-11 short gun. The final 20 delivered on 25 March 1941 were the latest T-34 Model 1941 with the longer 76mm F-34 gun. The 5th Tank Division was only the third Soviet tank division to receive the new tanks, and it was the only unit equipped with them in the Baltic Special Military District. Technical manuals were considered top secret and closely held, making training extremely difficult. Overall divisional tank strength fell from 292 to 268 tanks as a result of the swap of the T-34 for the worn-out BT-7 tanks. The 5th Tank Division did not receive any of the new KV heavy tanks.

A pair of BT-7 Model 1937 tanks of the 10th Tank Regiment knocked out during the fighting around the Kaniūkai bridgehead on 22 June 1941. The nearest tank has been hit in the turret bustle and the ensuing ammunition explosion has ripped off the turret rear. (NARA)

On 25 April 1941, Kurkin was appointed to take overall command of the 3rd Mechanized Corps, taking Rotmistrov with him to the corps headquarters. He was replaced by one the corps' staff officers, Colonel Fëdor F. Fëdorov, who was junior in rank for such a command role. Fëdorov's career record was not especially distinguished, and he had not yet attended a military academy, which was preferred for divisional commanders. The leadership positions through the division were filled by inexperienced officers one of two ranks below the usual standard. Only one of the eight tank battalions was commanded by a major and half were commanded by lieutenants, two grades below the standard. Of the personnel in staff positions, fewer than a quarter had completed secondary education. At the outset of the war, 68 per cent of Red Army platoon and company commanders had undergone only a five-month instruction course.

5th Tank Division (Colonel Fëdor F. Fëdorov)

9th Tank Regiment (Colonel Ivan P. Verkov)

> 1st Tank Battalion (Major Stepan I. Aksenov)
> 2nd Tank Battalion (Senior Lieutenant Ivan G. Verbitskiy)
> 3rd Tank Battalion (Senior Lieutenant Samuil Kh. Dobrusin)
> 4th Tank Battalion (Captain Ivan M. Osipov)

10th Tank Regiment (Colonel Terentiy Ya. Bogdanov)

> 1st Tank Battalion (Captain Petr E. Komagorov)
> 2nd Tank Battalion (Captain Aleksey Z. Lapshinov)
> 3rd Tank Battalion (Senior Lieutenant Ivan I. Voronin)
> 4th Tank Battalion (Senior Lieutenant Stepan T. Kesarev)

5th Moto-Rifle Regiment (Colonel Sergey I. Karpetyan)

> 1st Rifle Battalion (Major Ivan T. Mayorov)
> 2nd Rifle Battalion (Senior Lieutenant Fedor V. Yermolayev)
> 3rd Rifle Battalion (Captain Shalka A. Sodzhayev)

5th Howitzer Artillery Regiment (Major Vasiliy M. Komarov)

5th Separate Anti-Aircraft Battalion (Captain Mikhail I. Shilov)

5th Reconnaissance Battalion (Captain Fedor V. Korshunov)

5th Pontoon-Bridge Battalion (Captain Aleksey A. Ponomarenko)

5th Separate Signals Battalion (Major Georgiy Ya. Isayev)

5th Motor Transport Battalion (Captain Aleksandr I. Bulygin)

5th Repair-Recovery Battalion (Lieutenant-Colonel Ivan V. Polukarov)

5th Medical Battalion (Dr Aleksey A. Kochetov)

3rd Mechanized Corps armoured vehicles, 22 June 1941					
	Corps HQ	2nd Tank Division	5th Tank Division	84th Moto-Rifle Division	Total
BA-10	5	63	56	42	166
BA-20	5	27	20	6	58
BT-7	0	116	170	145	431
KT	0	12	0	0	12
KV-1	0	32	0	0	32
KV-2	0	19	0	0	19
T-26	0	19	18	4	41
T-28	0	27	30	0	57
T-34	0	0	50	0	50

5th Tank Division armoured vehicles, 22 June 1941					
	9th Tank Regiment	**10th Tank Regiment**	**5th Moto-Rifle Regiment**	**Other***	**Total**
BT-7	53	89	19	9	170
T-26	7	7	0	4	18
T-28	27	1	0	2	30
T-34	50	0	0	0	50
Armoured cars	20	20	18	18	76

* Includes divisional units, training tanks and vehicles in repair.

Most of the enlisted men had arrived with the new wave of draftees in early 1941 and were only partially trained. The 5th Tank Division received awards in 1940 for the proficiency of its troops largely due to the experience gained in the marches into Poland and Lithuania. By 1941, many of these troops had fulfilled their military obligations and returned to civilian life.

Basic training at the division's base lasted two months. After this, tank-crew specialists such as drivers were given a further six months' training, while tank commander/gunners who received a sergeant's rank were given a further ten months' training. On average, 73 per cent of the enlisted men in the mechanized corps were new draftees in service six months since the start of 1941, 27 per cent were in their second year of duty and less than 1 per cent were in their third year, mainly as NCOs. The Red Army did not have a professional NCO class, and so most NCOs in the division were little better trained than the average soldier. The Red Army tended to use junior lieutenants rather than NCOs for many tasks, but they lacked the experience of NCOs in Western armies. Officers accounted for about 9 per cent of Red Army personnel compared to about 4 per cent in the German Army due to this fundamental organizational difference.

Specialized training in the 5th Tank Division at the time of the German invasion was inadequate. For example, of the 564 men in the 5th Tank Division in late April 1941 assigned as tank and vehicle drivers, 210 (37 per cent) had less than two hours of driving experience, 204 (36 per cent) had ten hours or less, and only 151 (27 per cent) had more than ten hours. Part of the reason for this was the limited durability of the tanks. To save wear and tear on the tanks, a small fraction were used for training while the rest remained in storage. So in the case of the 50 T-34 tanks in the 5th Tank Division, only six were used for training, considerably slowing the training process. These few tanks quickly wore out and by mid-May 1941, one-third of the 3rd Mechanized Corps' T-34 training tanks were inoperable due to worn main clutches caused by driver error.

THE STRATEGIC SITUATION

The battles in this book took place in the contested border region between East Prussia and Lithuania on the axis Suwałki–Alytus–Vilnius. After regaining its independence from Russia in the wars of 1919–20, Lithuania came under threat again in 1939. Germany took control of the Klaipeda region in March 1939. After the defeat of Poland in 1939, the contested Vilnius region was turned over from Poland to Lithuania by Stalin. The absorption of Lithuania into the Soviet Union in June 1940 moved the Soviet border up to the eastern border of Germany.

Stalin initiated a programme of political repression to crush Lithuanian nationalism through political arrests and the large-scale deportations of civic leaders to the GULAG concentration camps. The Lithuanian Army was incorporated into the Red Army, though the Lithuanian units remained separate under new Soviet designations. The Soviet actions in 1939–41 were deeply resented in Lithuania and the population was pro-German and anti-Russian at the time of the 1941 campaign – something that would have consequences for the defence of the Soviet frontier in June 1941. The German Abwehr intelligence service had an easy time recruiting disgruntled Lithuanian Army officers in the months before the war, providing a detailed intelligence picture of deployments in

45

Lithuania. These were supplemented with frequent aerial intrusions by German reconnaissance aircraft over the border regions.

Owing to the fluidity of the national boundaries in the preceding century, there were no coherent border defences in 1941. Imperial Russia had constructed fortified garrisons in Lithuania in the late 19th century, including two in Alytus. Following the 1940 absorption of the Baltic States, the Red Army began construction of forward border defences, sometimes called the 'Molotov Line'. Construction in the Alytus area did not start until 4 June 1941. The 48th Alytus Fortified District (48-i Alitusskiy ukreplenniy rayon) stretched 16km from Kalvarija southwards to Kapčiamiestis. The district was supposed to include five main strongpoints with 273 pillboxes and other structures. At the time of the German invasion, only 20 structures had been built, and only a single unit, the 180th Separate Machine-Gun Battalion, had been assigned to the district.

Although Nazi Germany and Soviet Russia were ostensibly allies under the Molotov–Ribbentrop Pact, there were few illusions on either side that this alliance would endure. In February 1941, the Baltic Special Military District held a wargame simulating an attack on an 'Eastern' defender on the Suwałki–Vilnius axis by a 'Western' opponent enjoying 3-to-1 superiority in infantry and 6-to-1 superiority in tanks starting on 18 June. This closely mimicked the actual German operation on 22 June 1941. During the wargame, the 'Eastern' forces routed the 'Western' forces, driving them back to the frontier by 5 July 1941. The actual results of the German invasion that summer were markedly different from the wishful thinking embodied in the wargame.

Soviet preparations for the anticipated German attack were heavily influenced by the perceptions and delusions of Joseph Stalin. The Soviet leader was obsessed with the idea that Germany would trick Moscow into a conflict by staging a minor border incident; the resulting Soviet response would provide the pretext for an invasion. Stalin himself had used provocations in the Baltic States as a pretext for the Soviet occupation in 1940. Due to this fixation, Stalin was adamant that the Red Army should minimize its forces in the immediate border zones aside from the usual NKVD border-guard detachments. Appreciating the unpreparedness of the Red Army, he was anxious to postpone a conflict for as long as possible.

The Red Army had ample evidence that the Wehrmacht was planning to invade the Soviet Union in June 1941, and this was especially evident to the units that were stationed along the former Lithuanian and Polish borders. German aircraft frequently overflew the border, and the Red Air Force did nothing to stop them due to Stalin's orders. It was difficult for the Germans to hide their units. For example, in the days before the start of Operation *Barbarossa*, 7. Panzer-Division had its units stretched along the Suwałki–Kalvarija road for nearly 60km. Stalin prevented the Red Army from taking appropriate steps to prepare for the anticipated German invasion. As a result, the German invasion on 22 June 1941 provides an unusual case study of a successful strategic surprise even though there was no tactical surprise. (This odd situation is very evident in the orders and reports of the Baltic Military District in the days before the war. These can be found in several issues of *The Journal of Soviet Military Studies*, starting with Vol. 4, No. 4, December 1991.)

The Red Army did not have an accurate perception of German operational goals in 1941. There was a presumption that the focus of any German attack would be into

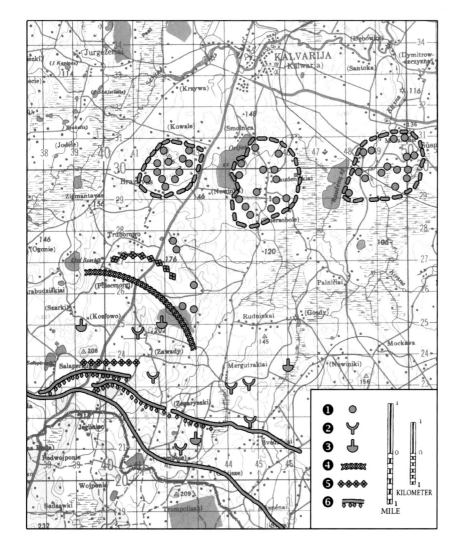

This map, based on 7. Panzer-Division's *Kriegstagebuch* (war diary), shows the Soviet Molotov Line defences on the road from the German border (lower left) to Kalvarija. There were three fortified strongpoints south of the city under construction but not complete at the time of the invasion. There were modest defence works along the frontier. The legend indicates: (**1**) bunker; (**2**) machine-gun nest; (**3**) observation bunker; (**4**) barbed wire; (**5**) anti-tank trap; (**6**) trenches and foxholes.

Ukraine, and as a result, the bulk of the Soviet mechanized force was deployed in that region. In fact, the Germans placed the major concentration of their Panzer force in the north, emanating out of East Prussia towards the Lithuanian frontier, as is evident from a quick glance at the accompanying map here. From a tactical perspective, this was due to the intention to encircle and destroy the large concentration of Red Army forces of the Western Special Military District that had been forward-deployed in a very vulnerable configuration in occupied eastern Poland after the 1939 campaign. From an operational perspective, Heeresgruppe Nord planned to strike northward along the Baltic towards Leningrad, while the northern wing of Heeresgruppe Mitte could strike towards Moscow.

Owing to Stalin's anxieties about provoking the Wehrmacht, the Red Army was constrained in deploying its units close to the German border until the last moment. Soviet units were under strict instructions not to engage German troops without prior permission from higher authorities. In the event of any such German provocations, the forward troops in Lithuania were to inform the Baltic Special Military District

headquarters by radio using the codeword *Slon* (elephant). Only after the headquarters had decided how to react were the divisions to open their prepared packets holding the war mobilization plans. A top-secret Baltic Special Military District instruction to the forward field armies at 0225hrs on the morning of 22 June 1941 warned that 'The mission for our units is not to respond to a single German provocation since it may cause enormous complications. At the same time, our units must be in complete combat readiness to meet and rout a surprise German attack.' These contradictory and ambiguous instructions interfered with a timely response to the German invasion in the first hours of the war.

As the likelihood of war increased, emergency measures began to be implemented. On 14 June 1941, Soviet security forces began a massive repression programme against Lithuanian civic leaders, deporting about 17,000 people to the Siberian GULAG camps. In the immediate border area, civilian populations were moved back about 5km from the frontier and on 20 June 1941, civilian horses in the border area were taken under control by the Red Army. On 18–19 June 1941, the 5th Tank Division and several other units in Lithuania were ordered to depart from their garrisons and take up tactical positions. Officers of the 5th Tank Division began moving their families from their garrisons in Alytus back into the Soviet Union.

Hitler's choice of Sunday 22 June 1941 as the date for the start of Operation *Barbarossa* had its historical echo in the fact that Napoleon had crossed the Neman River on 22 June 1812 near Kaunas at the start of his campaign against Russia. This sector of the East Prussian–Lithuanian frontier was covered by small detachments of the NKVD's 107th 'Mariampol' Border Detachment, a battalion-sized unit. The Border Guard troops were mainly stationed at border crossings for the usual customs purposes with a modest secondary defence mission. Red Army units facing the Wehrmacht in the Alytus sector were unusually weak. This sector was the responsibility of the 29th Territorial Rifle Corps of the 11th Army, a nominally Lithuanian formation formed from two infantry divisions of the pre-war Lithuanian Army. Since Moscow did not have great faith in the Lithuanian forces, regular Soviet units were deployed in this sector in the days before the invasion. Facing XXXIX. Armeekorps (mot.) was only a single, partially deployed unit, the 126th Rifle Division. This unit had been stationed in Latvia on the Baltic coast and its commander was not alerted until the afternoon of 18 June 1941 to prepare to move the division by rail to the Lithuanian temporary capital of Kaunas. Most of the division reached only as far as the south-western outskirts of Kaunas before war broke out.

In the early-morning hours of 22 June 1941, Baltic Special Military District headquarters ordered the 11th Army to dispatch a force from the 126th Rifle Division to Kalvarija to block the main road from the frontier to the Neman River crossings at Alytus. At least on paper, three battalions of the division reached the frontier on the night of 21/22 June. Efforts to concentrate anti-tank mines in special depots near the border were supposed to be completed on 21 June 1941, but actual mine laying along the frontier was not authorized until 0225hrs on 22 June 1941 and so never took place in any systematic fashion.

Defence of the Alytus bridges was nominally the responsibility of the 7th Company, 84th Regiment, 9th Division of the NKVD Border Troops. This was in fact a very small force numbering only 63 lightly armed soldiers. The bridges also had 37mm anti-aircraft guns of the 5th Air Defence Battalion. There is some controversy regarding any pre-war preparations to demolish the bridges. The Baltic Special Military District instructed its engineer units to draw up plans for such demolitions by 21 June 1941, but there is no evidence that any actual preparation had taken place. Instructions to place explosives on the bridges do not appear to have been issued until after the German attack on 22 June 1941.

As mentioned before, on 18 June 1941, the Baltic Special Military District ordered the 5th Tank Division to leave its peacetime garrison in Alytus and deploy on the east bank of the Neman River. The division was detached from the 3rd Mechanized Corps on 21 June by the commander of the Baltic Special Military District and subordinated to the 11th Army. It was tasked with covering the junction between the North-western Front and Western Front by defending a 30km stretch of the Neman River. The division was not expected to actually hold a defensive line. Rather, it was envisaged as a mobile counter-attack force that would repulse any penetration of the forward infantry defences. The problem with this plan was that there were really no defences between the East Prussian border and the Neman River due to the belated deployment of the 126th Rifle Division.

7. Panzer-Division's immediate objective for the first day of the war was to seize the bridges over the Neman River at Alytus leading to Vilnius. There were two principal bridges near Alytus: the bridge that ran through the town and the Kaniūkai bridge south of town. A third railway bridge immediately south of the town had not been reconstructed since World War I. German intelligence was well informed about these bridges since the original Russian bridges had been demolished by the retreating Tsarist Army in 1915 and reconstructed by the Kaiser's army afterwards.

PzKpfw 38(t) deployed for Operation *Barbarossa*, 22 June 1941

Division	Panzergruppe	Corps	PzKpfw 38(t)	PzBefWg 38(t)	Total
7. Panzer-Division	3	XXXIX.	167	7	174
8. Panzer-Division	4	LVI.	118	7	125
12. Panzer-Division	3	LVII.	109	8	117
19. Panzer-Division	3	LVII.	110	11	121
20. Panzer-Division	3	XXXIX.	121	2	123
Total			625	35	**660**

BT tank deployment in Soviet mechanized corps on 22 June 1941

Corps	Military district	BT-2	BT-5	BT-7	Total
1st Mechanized Corps	Leningrad	0	169	383	552
10th Mechanized Corps	Leningrad	157	142	62	361
3rd Mechanized Corps	Baltic	0	0	410	410
12th Mechanized Corps	Baltic	0	0	239	239
6th Mechanized Corps	Western	41	125	250	416
11th Mechanized Corps	Western	2	44	0	46
13th Mechanized Corps	Western	2	0	13	15
14th Mechanized Corps	Western	2	4	0	6
17th Mechanized Corps	Western	0	0	24	24
20th Mechanized Corps	Western	0	0	13	13
2nd Mechanized Corps	Odessa	0	0	354	354
18th Mechanized Corps	Odessa	17	14	75	106
7th Mechanized Corps	Moscow	39	0	190	229
4th Mechanized Corps	Kiev	0	0	297	297
8th Mechanized Corps	Kiev	17	0	260	277
9th Mechanized Corps	Kiev	24	61	90	175
15th Mechanized Corps	Kiev	0	0	471	471
16th Mechanized Corps	Kiev	0	42	126	168
22nd Mechanized Corps	Kiev	5	0	173	178
24th Mechanized Corps	Kiev	0	0	5	5
25th Mechanized Corps	Kharkov	0	0	0	0
27th Mechanized Corps	Central Asian	0	23	0	23
28th Mechanized Corps	Caucasus	4	14	0	18
5th Mechanized Corps	Baikal	11	161	502	674
29th Mechanized Corps	Baikal	0	161	478	639
30th Mechanized Corps	Far East	2	29	367	398
Total		323	989	4,782	**6,094**

OPPOSITE Operation *Barbarossa* in Lithuania, 22 June 1941.

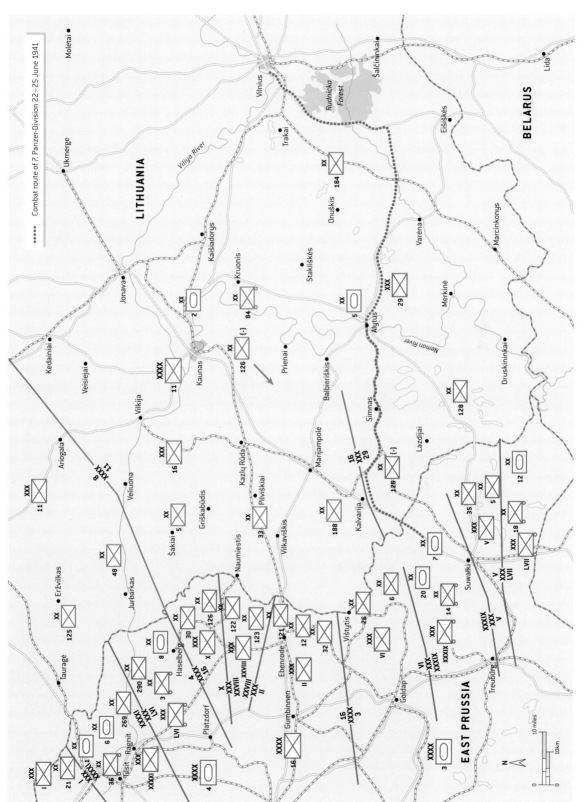

COMBAT

The attack along the Suwałki–Alytus axis by XXXIX. Armeekorps (mot.) began at 0305hrs on 22 June 1941. 7. Panzer-Division formed the spearhead of the attack; Panzer-Regiment 21 of 20. Panzer-Division was attached to 7. Panzer-Division as reinforcement and instructed to follow behind the division's march groups. While television documentaries about Operation *Barbarossa* tend to dramatize the opening phase of the invasion, showing massive barrages of heavy artillery along the frontier,

The Neman River bridge at Kaniūkai in June 1941 as viewed from the eastern bank looking south-west. The eastern bank had high, forested cliffs overlooking the river. (NARA)

This PzKpfw 38(t) of III./PzRgt 25 ran over a mine outside Alytus on 22 June 1941. Passing to the left is a Krupp L2H143 truck, the standard mode of transportation for the *Schützen-Regiment*. (NARA)

7. Panzer-Division had its field artillery in place for fire missions but did not use it until there was a tactical need to do so. Infiltration was regarded as a preferable tactic.

Leading 7. Panzer-Division's attack was one of its two motorized-infantry units, Schützen-Regiment 7, which crossed the border and reached Height 198 around 0325hrs 'against weak resistance'. A platoon-sized unit of the NKVD 107th Border Detachment on the Suwałki–Kalvarija road was brushed aside. This followed the usual German doctrine of using the infantry to secure the breakthrough and holding back the Panzers for the exploitation. Since there were no German infantry divisions in this sector, 7. Panzer-Division had to use its own infantry for this initial mission. Panzer-Flamm-Abteilung 101 had been attached to the division to deal with any bunkers near the frontier. In the event, none were encountered and so the flamethrower tanks remained with Panzer-Regiment 25.

Schützen-Regiment 6 moved up next, proceeding on either side of the Suwałki–Kalvarija road to the village of Zovoda by 0345hrs, still encountering little resistance. Although the 126th Rifle Division had sent forward three battalions to set up an initial defence of the border, there was no evidence of these troops in the early-morning hours. The road towards the Neman River turns abruptly eastward before reaching the town of Kalvarija, so there was no need to occupy this town immediately. Instead, the German divisional artillery began fire strikes against the town starting at 0357hrs to cover the left flank as 7. Panzer-Division began to turn eastwards towards the town of Simnas.

The Soviet 48th Fortification District had erected two anti-tank ditches and a barbed-wire barrier across the Suwałki–Kalvarija road and so combat engineers from Panzer-Pionier-Bataillon 58 preceded the tank columns to facilitate a quick passage. The essence of Blitzkrieg was mobility and speed, and the Panzer columns stayed on the roads as long as possible since it was faster than cross-country travel. As the columns from Panzer-Regiment 25 proceeded past the border around dawn, German reconnaissance aircraft reported that there were few if any Soviet troops evident along the road. There was some skirmishing with Soviet infantry south of Kalvarija after

The 10th Tank Regiment sent a patrol over to the west bank of the Neman River on the approaches to Alytus where they ran into a scout party from Gefechtsgruppe *Rothenburg*. This BA-10A armoured car was knocked out in this preliminary skirmish. (NARA)

dawn, presumably the lead elements of the arriving 126th Rifle Division, but the spearhead of Panzer-Regiment 25 reached the town by 0900hrs.

With the path to the Neman River surprisingly devoid of serious defences, 7. Panzer-Division's motorcycle unit, Kradschützen-Bataillon 7, sent motorcycle teams further up the road, both to scout and to seize important terrain objectives such as bridges. The East Prussian–Lithuanian border was full of small rivers and streams, swamps and wooded areas and so there were numerous potential bottlenecks along the road that needed to be secured. Schützen-Brigade 7 followed behind Panzer-Regiment 25 and cleared and occupied Kalvarija in the early morning. The division established its forward headquarters at the road-junction south of the town at 1050hrs.

The main Soviet air base in the region, at Varėna, south-east of Alytus, was attacked by the Luftwaffe, and at least two I-15bis biplane fighters were downed over the air base by a German fighter sweep at about 1030hrs. The Luftwaffe began air attacks on Alytus, with the first major attack at 1137hrs. The only significant military damage was the destruction of much of the equipment of the 5th Tank Division's pontoon-bridge battalion that was still located in the northern garrison.

On hearing news of the German invasion earlier in the morning, the 5th Tank Division commander, Colonel Fëdor Fëdorov, attempted to rally his scattered division. One motor-infantry battalion from Colonel Sergei I. Karpetyan's 5th Moto-Rifle Regiment was sent back into Alytus to defend the city bridge. One battalion of Colonel Ivan P. Verkov's 9th Tank Regiment was already in position to defend the northern bridge from the eastern side, and a second battalion was sent to reinforce it. Colonel Terentiy Ya. Bogdanov's 10th Tank Regiment was ordered to send tanks to defend the Kaniūkai road bridge south of Alytus. The 10th Tank Regiment sent a small detachment of BA-10 armoured cars to scout the western bank of the Neman River where they engaged in a skirmish with German troops, probably from Kradschützen-Bataillon 7, losing at least one BA-10 in the process.

OPPOSITE The battle for the Alytus bridges, 22 June 1941.

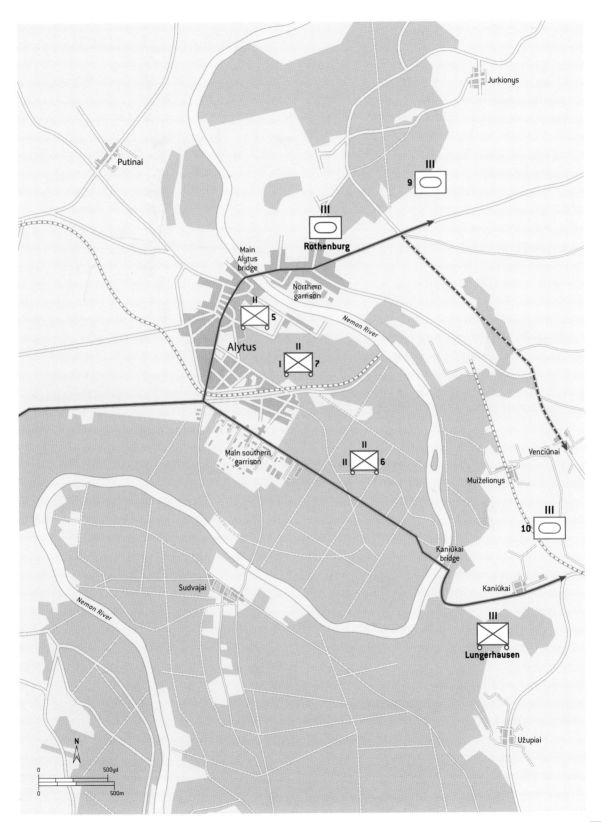

Jurkionys

Putinai

III
9

III
Rothenburg

Main
Alytus
bridge

Northern
garrison

Neman River

II
5

Alytus

II
I 7

Main southern
garrison

II
II 6

Venčiūnai

Muiželionys

III
10

Kaniūkai
bridge

Sudvajai

Kaniūkai

Neman River

III
Lungerhausen

Užupiai

N

0   500yd

0   500m

55

THE BATTLE FOR THE ALYTUS BRIDGES

7. Panzer-Division's plan was to seize the northern Alytus town bridge using a *Gefechtsgruppe* (combat group) under Oberst Karl Rothenburg based around Panzer-Regiment 25 reinforced with Panzer-Aufklärungs-Abteilung 37 and the flamethrower tanks of Panzer-Flamm-Abteilung 101, while a second *Gefechtsgruppe* under Oberst Carl-Hans Lungershausen based around the motorcycle troops of Kradschützen-Bataillon 7 would seize the Kaniūkai road bridge. There was some confusion about the routes leading into Alytus since the signage was in Russian and Lithuanian. The Panzer columns were moving very quickly in the midst of billowing clouds of dust. At a key 'Y' intersection west of the town, some of the German sub-units ended up making the wrong turn. For example, II./PzRgt 25 ended up at the Kaniūkai road bridge instead of its intended objective at the northern bridge. This proved fortuitous later in the afternoon when the southern bridgehead was hit by a major Soviet tank attack.

A few companies of the 5th Moto-Rifle Regiment arrived in Alytus prior to the German spearheads and deployed their defences to cover the roads approaching town. The town was divided on either side of the Neman River, and at the time had a population slightly under 10,000. A few 37mm anti-aircraft guns of the 5th Air Defence Battalion were already in the town for their normal air-defence mission, and they were ordered to prepare to deal with ground targets. The Soviet infantry also had a few 76mm regimental guns. These did not have armour-piercing ammunition, but their high-explosive rounds could damage the thinly armoured German tanks when used at close range.

As the German columns approached, fighting broke out in the outskirts of town shortly before noon. The lead elements of Panzer-Regiment 25 proceeded in haste down the main street towards the bridge, largely ignoring the Soviet defences. During

A view of Alytus during the approach of elements of Gefechtsgruppe *Rothenburg* to the town on the morning of 22 June 1941. Smoke already rises from fighting in the town. (NARA)

the ensuing fighting, the Soviet anti-aircraft gun crews claimed to have knocked out 14 German tanks and the 76mm regimental guns a further 16 German tanks. Judging from German accounts, which suggest that there was very limited fighting before the bridges were captured, these figures were a gross exaggeration.

The leading German tanks, a mixture from I./PzRgt 25 and III./PzRgt 25, approached the northern bridge at about noon against only light resistance. According to 7. Panzer-Division's war diary, both Alytus bridges were in German hands by 1245hrs. There are numerous, contradictory Russian accounts explaining why the bridges were not ready for demolition. The Soviet 4th Separate Engineer Regiment of the Baltic Special Military District had been instructed to prepare the Alytus bridges for demolitions by 1400hrs, but the pace of the German advance was completely unanticipated. One of the explosives teams was captured by the Germans before reaching the bridge, and the bridges were in German hands before the other demolition team arrived. 7. Panzer-Division also captured the ferry site at Nemunaitis, 7km south of Alytus, which was subsequently used to assemble a pontoon bridge over the Neman River. One of the officers of III./PzRgt 25 recalled the scene at the northern bridge as the first column of German tanks began to pass over to the eastern side:

> After about twenty tanks of III./Pz.Rgt.25 had crossed the northern bridge, the twenty-first tank was hit by a Soviet tank. It was in a well concealed position near the bridge and had not been detected by the German tanks. The commander of the German tank, a senior lieutenant, was killed. The Soviet tank rushed back to its own lines, passing by the thirty German tanks scattered through the area. Several (PzKpfw 38t) tanks, including mine, tried to destroy the enemy tank with our 37mm guns. These attempts had no effect on the T-34 which was our first encounter with this type.

Judging from surviving photographs, the German tank knocked out on the Alytus bridge was a PzKpfw IV. Some Russian accounts credit this incident to the T-34 tank commanded by Sergeant Makogon, who later claimed to have knocked out a total of six German tanks during the fighting near Alytus on 22 June.

German expansion of the northern bridgehead was frustrated by a concentration of tanks of Verkov's 9th Tank Regiment. Senior Lieutenant Ivan G. Verbitskiy's 2nd Tank Battalion had dug in most of its T-34 tanks on the eastern bank of the river in the days before the invasion. This unit was reinforced that morning with the arthritic T-28 tanks of Major Stepan I. Aksenov's 1st Tank Battalion, 9th Tank Regiment. Aksenov's unit charged into the German columns and claimed to have knocked out five German tanks in the ensuing melee, a few by ramming the small PzKpfw 38(t) with the much larger T-28 medium tank. At least one German staff car was run over and crushed by a BT-7 tank.

In the southern bridgehead, II./PzRgt 25 attempted to expand the bridgehead towards the village of Kaniūkai, but had six tanks knocked out by tank-gun fire from the hull-down BT-7 tanks under Captain Novikov that were well camouflaged on the forested cliffs overlooking the river. This was the lead battle-group from Bogdanov's 10th Tank Regiment, with more tanks arriving as the day wore on.

Fëdorov fed Soviet tank companies into the battle as they arrived on the scene. A coordinated Soviet tank counter-attack was launched at about 1400hrs against the

OVERLEAF Much of the fighting for the Alytus bridges on 22 June took part on the eastern side of the town where the urban congestion gave way to the rural countryside. The PzKpfw 38(t) tanks of Panzer-Regiment 25 encountered the BT-7 tanks of the 5th Tank Division in a series of small but violent skirmishes. The main advantage enjoyed by Panzer-Regiment 25 was the battle experience gained during the fighting in France in 1940. By June 1941, the tankers of 7. Panzer-Division had become acclimated to combat. In contrast, the Soviet crews of the 5th Tank Division were mostly new recruits who had barely mastered the most basic skills of operating their tanks. To make matters worse, the BT-7 commanders had very limited vision from inside their tanks, and were overwhelmed with the tasks of operating the main gun as well as directing their inexperienced crews. German tank crews often recalled that the Soviet tanks tended to stumble around the battlefield, seemingly without any central direction or focus. This was as a result of a combination of limited training and the poor situational awareness inherent in the BT-7 turret design.

A T-28 medium tank of Major Stepan I. Aksenov's 1st Tank Battalion, 9th Tank Regiment, knocked out in the fighting at the northern bridgehead near Alytus on the afternoon of 22 June. These tanks were largely worn out from previous operations in Poland in 1939, and many broke down before reaching combat. (NARA)

northern bridge in which the BT-7 and T-34 tanks made repeated attacks against the German positions without infantry or artillery support. The piecemeal attacks were shot up by the stationary PzKpfw 38(t) and PzKpfw IV tanks. The unanticipated presence of large numbers of the heavily armoured T-34 tanks posed a real problem for the Panzer crews since neither the 3.7cm gun on the PzKpfw 38(t) nor the short 7.5cm gun on the PzKpfw IV could defeat the T-34 in a frontal engagement. Fortunately, a single battery of 10.5cm field guns had been attached to Gefechtsgruppe *Rothenburg*, and the field guns of I./AR 78 played a vital role in dealing with the T-34 tanks. Although the guns could not penetrate the T-34 armour, the impact of a 10.5cm high-explosive round at close range could inflict enough damage to stop the tank. The 10.5cm projectile could easily blow away tracks or road-wheels; and even if it failed to penetrate the armour, a solid hit would cause the inner face of the armour plate to spall away into the interior of the tank, injuring or killing the crew.

In spite of the 44 new T-34 tanks in the 9th Tank Regiment committed to the day's battle, they did not have a decisive influence on the fight for the Alytus town bridge. The Soviet tank attacks were relentless but not especially well coordinated. The Soviet tank crews did not have good situational awareness, and seemed to stumble around with no central direction. There is also reason to believe that the T-34 tanks had little or no armour-piercing ammunition. The Soviet tanks were picked off one-by-one by the German tanks and field guns. The poor performance of the 5th Tank Division during this attack suggests inexperience and poor training at all levels of command.

Oberleutnant Horst Ohrloff of 11./PzRgt 25, who was decorated with the Knight's Cross of the Iron Cross on 27 July 1941, described the day's tank battle as 'The hardest combat ever conducted by 7. Panzer-Division in World War II'. The Soviet attack was brave but amateurish, and the regiment commander, Oberst Karl Rothenburg, characterized the battle as 'the hardest fight of my life'. In spite of the intensity of the fight for the northern Alytus bridge, actual German tank casualties were modest. Only five tanks were written off as total losses, though others were disabled during the fighting.

The Soviet counter-attack increased the pressure on the southern Kaniūkai bridgehead, which was being held by the Panhard armoured cars of Panzer-Aufklärungs-Abteilung 37, a single infantry company and a single tank battalion. After Gefechtsgruppe *Rothenburg* repulsed the Soviet tank attacks at the northern bridgehead, it pushed southwards along the east bank of the Neman River to relieve the smaller and weaker Gefechtsgruppe *Lungershausen* at the southern Kaniūkai bridgehead. At 1530hrs, Rothenburg reported back to the division headquarters that the Soviet counter-attacks had been smashed.

At about 1710hrs, Gefechtsgruppe *Schmidt* (Panzer-Regiment 21 of 20. Panzer-Division) arrived in Alytus and deployed near the northern city bridge. This regiment was ordered to take over the defence of the northern Alytus bridgehead and to hand over one-third of its tank-gun ammunition to replenish the badly depleted stocks of Panzer-Regiment 25. The battered and bloody III./PzRgt 25 was pulled out of the line to serve as a reserve in the event that the Soviet tank attacks resumed that evening.

During the day's fighting, Panzer-Regiment 25 claimed to have knocked out 70 Soviet tanks while I./AR 78 claimed 12 and the Panhard armoured cars of Panzer-Aufklärungs-Abteilung 37 claimed three for a total of 85 Soviet tanks. German sources listed their own total losses for the day as 11 tanks, consisting of four PzKpfw IVs and seven light tanks, mainly PzKpfw 38(t), and at least one of the Flammpanzer II. Additional tanks were knocked out or damaged, but recovered. Casualties in Panzer-Regiment 25 were two officers killed and 12 wounded; nine enlisted men killed and 16 wounded. Bronius Aušrotas, a Lithuanian officer serving with Wehrmacht intelligence, witnessed the scene near the Kaniūkai bridge a few days after the battle:

After passing over the Nieman [Neman] bridge, we drove up a steep hill a hundred meters or more. When we reached the top of the hill, we saw a tank grave-yard. On both

A view of the battlefield on the east bank of the Neman River after the 22 June battle with two knocked-out PzKpfw 38(t) visible. The damage to the turret of the nearest PzKpfw 38(t) suggests that it was hit by a 76mm high-explosive round. (NARA)

sides of the road leading to Valkininku [Valkininkai] were graves with crosses identifying the dead soldiers. We stopped the car and got out, counting the number of our own tanks and those of the enemy. I counted about 30 Soviet T-34 tanks and other types. The German Panzer tanks of various models numbered about a dozen.

The fighting around Alytus decreased later in the day. Early that evening at about 1840hrs, Panzer-Regiment 21 engaged some Soviet tanks in the woods north-east of Alytus near the small airfield north of the town. The Soviet 5th Moto-Rifle Regiment disengaged from the fighting inside Alytus and withdrew to the east bank of the Neman River after nightfall. By the end of the day, Soviet tank losses were quite heavy, totalling about 90 tanks. The heaviest losses were suffered by Verkov's 9th Tank Regiment that defended the northern Alytus bridge. It lost 73 of its 117 tanks (62 percent) including 27 of its 44 T-34 tanks, 16 of its 28 T-28 medium tanks and 30 of its 45 BT-7. Most of the T-28 tanks that survived the afternoon battle were abandoned late in the day due to mechanical problems. Soviet accounts indicate that a significant proportion of the day's tank losses were due to German air attacks, though this is not reflected in German accounts. It is possible that the 5th Tank Division lost more tanks in the rear areas that were not counted by 7. Panzer-Division that day. Recent Russian accounts suggest that about half of the day's tank losses were due to mechanical breakdowns and other mishaps, often during the course of the fighting. Photographs taken after the battle show a number of Soviet tanks that appear to have become trapped after driving off the road into ditches and obstructions, a consequence of poor training.

A PzKpfw IV Ausf E of III./PzRgt 25 knocked out during the fighting on the east bank of the Neman River near Alytus. A total of four PzKpfw IV were knocked out in the day's fighting. (NARA)

A BT-7 Model 1937 of the 10th Tank Regiment knocked out in the fighting near the Kaniūkai bridgehead on 22 June 1941. The white invasion cross from the occupation of Lithuania in 1940 is still evident on the turret hatch. The BT-7 Model 1937 was soon labelled the 'Mickey Mouse tank' by German tankers due to its appearance when its twin turret hatches were open. (NARA)

CONTESTING THE APPROACHES TO VILNIUS

South of the Alytus battlefield, LVII. Armeekorps (mot.) had pushed over the Neman River by seizing the bridge at Merkinė. In the lead was 12. Panzer-Division, followed by 18. Infanterie-Division (mot.). The drive continued after nightfall and at about 0200hrs on 23 June 1941, this force overran the Soviet air base at Varėna. This was reported mistakenly to Baltic Special Military District headquarters as a German 'airborne operation' and the 5th Tank Division was ordered to intervene. Fëdorov responded by leaving behind a rearguard of the 10th Tank Regiment near the Kaniūkai bridgehead, while the remainder of the regiment began a 40km night-march south-west towards the air base. A fight broke out around the Varėna airfield at about 0700hrs on 23 June, with the 10th Tank Regiment reporting that it had repulsed the German 'airborne' attack and retaken the airfield.

7. Panzer-Division spent most of the night of 22/23 June reconstituting its scattered forces and preparing for the next day's actions. The spearhead massed around the Kaniūkai bridge, since this connected to one of the few decent roads to the next day's objective, the city of Vilnius. The war-booty French Panhard armoured cars of Panzer-Aufklärungs-Abteilung 37 set out in the lead the next morning at about 0445hrs, followed by Panzer-Regiment 25 at about 0800hrs. While passing north of Varėna, Panzer-Regiment 25 became involved in another tank skirmish with elements of the 10th Tank Regiment which had responded to the 'airborne attack' at Varėna air base. Although not on the scale of the previous day's tank battles, sporadic tank skirmishes continued through the day. The 10th Tank Regiment and other elements of the 5th Tank Division gradually withdrew, some taking refuge in the Rudnicka (Rūdninkai)

Forest south-west of Vilnius while others moved south back into Belarus in the direction of Minsk.

The Rudnicka Forest proved to be a major impediment to the advance of 7. Panzer-Division on 23 June. The road through the forest was unpaved and sandy. This proved less of a problem for the PzKpfw 38(t) tanks of Panzer-Regiment 25 than for the following supply columns. The trucks soon became trapped along the sandy and swampy roads in the forest, clogging the main approach route to Vilnius. Many of the division's supply trucks were French war-booty, and these were not well suited to cross-country travel. By mid-afternoon, Panzer-Aufklärungs-Abteilung 37 and Panzer-Regiment 25 had secured the hills south and south-west of Vilnius, but were waiting for the division's infantry and artillery to catch up due to the traffic jams in the Rudnicka Forest. Generaloberst Hermann Hoth, the Panzergruppe 3 commander, visited the divisional staff late on Monday 23 June and instructed them to continue probing north-east of Vilnius to secure key roads and bridges, but to wait until the next morning before taking control of the city. In his memoirs, Hoth expressed disappointment in the slow pace of 7. Panzer-Division's advance on 23 June, especially when compared to the previous day's successes. The division's forward command post was established 13km south-west of Vilnius at about 0200hrs on Tuesday 24 June.

For all the difficulties endured by 7. Panzer-Division on Monday 23 June, the situation for the 5th Tank Division was infinitely worse. Battered by the previous day's fighting, the Soviet division had scattered into its constituent regiments. Coordination between its regiments proved impossible due to poor communication and dispersal after the Alytus fighting. To complicate matters further, the 5th Tank Division was now operating in the sector of the 29th Territorial Rifle Corps, the formation that had incorporated two-pre-war Lithuanian Army infantry divisions, the 179th and 184th Rifle divisions. The Lithuanian 184th Rifle Division was stationed on the road between Alytus and Vilnius and directly in the paths of the 5th Tank Division and the pursuing 7. Panzer-Division. On 23 June, the Lithuanian nationalist group Lietuvos Aktyvistų Frontas set up a provisional government and declared Lithuanian independence. On news of this, many of the Lithuanian troops began to mutiny.

A BT-7 Model 1937 of the 9th Tank Regiment abandoned in the Rudnicka Forest on 23 June 1941 during the retreat towards Vilnius. The tank appears to have broken both of its tracks. (NARA)

A T-34 Model 1941 of the 9th Tank Regiment knocked out or abandoned in the Rudnicka Forest south of Vilnius on 23 June 1941. This is the improved version of the T-34 with the longer 76mm F-34 gun, and first delivered to 5th Tank Division in March 1941. (NARA)

The city of Vilnius was weakly held by the 84th NKVD Regiment, the 12th Air Defence Brigade and parts of the 84th Moto-Rifle Division. After the Lithuanian troops of the 184th Rifle Division switched sides, many marched into Vilnius, taking control of much of the city by the morning of 24 June. Most Soviet troops abandoned Vilnius prior to the German advance into the city that day. Some of the Lithuanian troops actively fought against Soviet forces. So for example, the Soviet 5th Howitzer-Artillery Regiment was ambushed on several occasions during their retreat on 23 June by troops of the Lithuanian 184th Rifle Division.

As the surrounding countryside became more and more hostile to the retreating Red Army, many Soviet units began to make a dash towards the pre-war Soviet border and towards their old home bases in the Minsk area of Belarus. By this time, many of the division's tanks and trucks were running out of fuel. In this rural and agricultural region, there were few local fuel resources. Supplies could only be found across the pre-war Soviet border. Most of the 5th Tank Division's headquarters hastily retreated south of the Lithuanian frontier towards the Belarusian town of Oshmiany (now Ashmyany), while Colonel Fëdorov and his immediate operations staff remained with the 9th Tank Regiment in the Vilnius area for the time being. After the attack on German forces at the Varėna airfield, some elements of the 10th Tank Regiment joined with elements of other Soviet units retreating across the border into Belarus while other tank companies moved towards the Rudnicka Forest and Vilnius.

On the morning of 24 June 1941, a column of PzKpfw 38(t) tanks of 5./PzRgt 25 approached the Cathedral Basilica of St Stanislaus and St Vladislav, with the cathedral belfry evident in the background. The tank columns passed through the city quickly since they were assigned to secure river bridges further to the north-east that day. (NARA)

PzKpfw 38(t) SIGHTS

The Zielfernrohr 38(t) telescopic sight had two different reticle patterns. The early Czech pattern (shown here) had the horizontal deflection scale displayed in mils; the later reticle switched to the German pattern of deflection markings by using a series of small triangles. The unit of measure was a graduation (*Strich*) equalling 1m at 1,000m range, with the large centre triangle having sides of four graduations and the smaller triangle having sides of two graduations. The Czech style of reticles had the range calibrations as a 'staircase' on either side with armour-piercing on the left and high explosive on the right. The gunner introduced the super-elevation needed to compensate for range by dialling in the estimated range to target.

BT-7 SIGHTS

The BT-7 gunner had a choice of using two sights for aiming the 45mm 20K tank gun: the TOP-1 telescopic sight or the PT-1 Model 1932 tank periscopic sight. On the telescopic sight, the gunner had the choice of three reticles depending on the weapon being used. The reticle marked 'B' (*broniboyniy*) was for the armour-piercing ammunition, 'O' (*oskolochniy*) for high explosive and 'P' (*pulemet*) for the machine gun. The reticles were conventional, having a centre cross-hair aim point, a range scale, and below the cross-hairs, a deflection scale in mils. The reticle shown here is the one used with the periscopic sight for armour-piercing and was gradated out to the maximum range of 3,600m; the high explosive reticle had gradations out to 2,700m. Since the periscopic sight was traversable for observation purposes, the gunner first had to lock the sight along the boresight of the gun. The range scale is above the cross-hairs and is in hundreds of metres (hectometres); 6 = 600m. The gunner employed a dial on the sight to adjust for the needed super-elevation of the sight to compensate for range, with the selection indicated by the moving triangular indicator shown here in the 10 o'clock position for 600m.

The German advance into Vilnius began at about 0600hrs on Tuesday 24 June when the motorcycle troops of Kradschützen-Bataillon 7 seized the Vilnius-South airfield, capturing about 25 aircraft in the process. With the airfield secured, they proceeded into the city itself. After the departure of most of the Soviet troops, local civilians had decorated the buildings with Lithuanian flags, welcoming the Germans as liberators. Most of Panzer-Regiment 25 passed through the city starting at 1000hrs, intending to reach the bridge over the Viliya (Neris) River at Micháleshik (now Michalishki, Belarus). There were some skirmishes around Vilnius on 24 June, mainly encounters with surviving elements of the 5th Tank Division in the Rudnicka Forest. These Soviet tanks occasionally launched sorties out of the woods against the German columns moving towards Vilnius. For example, a few BT-7 tanks of the 10th Tank Regiment under Senior Sergeant Vedeneyev ambushed a German column and he claimed his tank knocked out five German tanks and four guns. Large numbers of Lithuanian troops also emerged out of the forest and volunteered to assist the German troops. The situation around Vilnius was fluid and chaotic for most of the day.

By the evening of 24 June, the only remaining element under Fëdorov's 5th Tank Division command was a battle-group with 15 tanks, 20 armoured cars and nine guns. During the day, this group retreated southwards to Molodechno in Belarus, 170km from Alytus, on the road between Vilnius and the Belarusian capital of Minsk. Fëdorov located the improvised 13th Army headquarters, where he met the head of the operations sections, Colonel Semion P. Ivanov. He lamented that 'the situation is hopeless and I will probably have to pay with my head'. He estimated that the losses to date had been about 70 per cent of the division's personnel strength, 150 tanks and about half of the division's trucks.

The 13th Army headquarters had only recently arrived in the area and had few resources at its disposal to meet the onrushing German forces. Most of the Western Special Military District units had been deployed further west in occupied Poland and the advance by Heeresgruppe Mitte threatened to encircle and trap them around Minsk. The 13th Army headquarters had been hastily thrown into the area in the hope of keeping the Minsk pocket open. The 13th Army commander, General-Major Petr M. Filatov, ordered Fëdorov to create a battle-group under Colonel Verkov of the 9th Tank Regiment using the surviving tanks at Molodechno along with the cadets of the Vilnius Infantry School and the 84th NKVD Regiment. Verkov's battle-group was instructed to push up the road from Molodechno towards Oshmiany, and then on to Vilnius. Unknown to Fëdorov, a surviving chunk of the 10th Tank Regiment, including 15 T-34 tanks and 14 T-26 tanks, had joined with the 37th Rifle Division of the 21st Rifle Corps, and also took part in this battle along the Vilnius–Minsk highway.

By this stage of the campaign, 7. Panzer-Division was heading across the old Soviet frontier as part of a larger effort by Heeresgruppe Mitte to encircle the three field armies of the Western Special Military District. A number of fortified border strongpoints of the old Stalin Line were assaulted and reduced by Schützen-Regiment 6 and Schützen-Regiment 7. This was one of the first times that the division had encountered a determined Soviet infantry defence.

The Soviet 13th Army, including the two surviving tank formations of the 5th Tank Division, launched their counter-attack from Molodechno on the morning of 25 June. Owing to a lack of communications between the assorted units, the counter-

FAR LEFT A PzKpfw 38(t) of II./ PzRgt 25 passes in front of the Cathedral Basilica of St Stanislaus and St Vladislav in the centre of Vilnius on 24 June 1941 after the capture of the city. This tank shows the style of large external turret stowage bins common on 7. Panzer-Division tanks. (NARA)

LEFT The last remaining 15 T-34 tanks of the 10th Tank Regiment took part in a counter-attack on the Minsk highway from Molodechno on 25 June 1941 in support of the 37th Rifle Division. They were all knocked out or abandoned. (NARA)

attack consisted of a series of small-scale actions along the highway. A BT-7 commanded by Senior Sergeant G.N. Naydin lay camouflaged in the woods near the road and claimed to have knocked out 10–12 German tanks during the day's fighting.

Oberst Erich von Unger's Schützen-Regiment 6 was in the lead that day due to the stiffening Soviet infantry defences that had been encountered along the old Lithuanian–Polish–Soviet frontier. 20. Panzer-Division, also equipped with PzKpfw 38(t) tanks, took part in the day's fighting towards Molodechno. The Soviet counter-attacks halted 7. Panzer-Division's advance that day. In the process, the surviving tanks of the 5th Tank Division were largely destroyed. As of 1600hrs, the 5th Tank Division had been reduced to five tanks and 12 other armoured vehicles. During the night of 25/26 June, a column from Panzer-Regiment 25 shot up a Soviet truck convoy carrying General-Major Filatov and the headquarters of the 13th Army; Filatov narrowly escaped. In spite of the delays on Wednesday 25 June, 7. Panzer-Division reached Minsk on 26 June, completing its part in the encirclement of the Minsk pocket.

At the end of Wednesday 25 June, the 13th Army reported that all that remained of the 5th Tank Division was three tanks and about 40 trucks and other vehicles. After various scattered elements were consolidated later in the area around Borisov (now Barysaŭ, Belarus), a report on 4 July 1941 put the division's remaining strength at 2,552 men, two BT-7 tanks, four BA-10 armoured cars and 261 trucks and other vehicles. The remnants of the division were ordered towards Kaluga where they were to be incorporated into a new tank division for the embryonic 14th Mechanized Corps.

By the conclusion of the Minsk encirclement and after a week of intense fighting, Panzer-Regiment 25 had suffered such severe attrition of its tanks that it had to temporarily disband one of its three battalions and consolidate its tanks in the other two battalions. Only about half of its PzKpfw 38(t) tanks were still functional; this was due more to mechanical breakdowns than to combat losses. Nevertheless, 7. Panzer-Division was still able to spearhead the drive for the Berezina River near Borisov over the course of the next several days, using I./PzRgt 25 as its spearhead.

STATISTICS AND ANALYSIS

The consequences of minor accidents, such as this one involving a PzKpfw 38(t) of 9./PzRgt 25 south of Kalvarija on the morning of 22 June 1941, depended on who controlled the battlefield at the end of the day. In the German case, this tank was recovered and continued in service with 7. Panzer-Division. Similar accidents involving Soviet tanks often led to the loss of the tank when it fell into German hands. (NARA)

The one-sided victories of the PzKpfw 38(t) tanks of 7. Panzer-Division against the BT-7 tanks of the 5th Tank Division were largely due to the broader issues of tactical experience and preparedness and not to technical advantages or disadvantages inherent in either vehicle. Stalin's misguided policies in the months before the war's outbreak exacerbated the Red Army's systemic problems. 7. Panzer-Division was able to secure its initial objectives on the Neman River with hardly any fighting due to Stalin's delays in permitting the reinforcement of the East Prussian–Lithuanian border.

From a purely technical standpoint, the Soviet counter-attack of the Neman bridgeheads on the afternoon of 22 June should have been a one-sided victory for the Red Army. The BT-7 tanks were similar in combat quality to the PzKpfw 38(t), and the Soviet forces had substantial numbers of the new T-34 tanks that had no equal on the German side. In spite of this technical advantage, the Soviet forces suffered disproportionate casualties during the 22 June tank battle at a ratio of about 8 to 1. More importantly, the Germans had gained

control of the vital Neman River crossings. The 5th Tank Division was largely destroyed as a coherent unit in the first day's fighting. Although the 5th Tank Division retained about half of its tank strength on 23 June, it never again seriously contested the advance of 7. Panzer-Division.

The 5th Tank Division largely evaporated after about three days of fighting. The division started the war with 268 tanks and lost about 90 tanks in the initial battles on Sunday 22 June, leaving about 180. Two days later, on Tuesday 24 June, Fëdorov estimated that the division had lost 150 tanks up to that point, implying that about 120 remained. Only two battle-groups were still operational on that date, however, with a total of about 45 tanks. By Wednesday 25 June, the division strength report indicated that only three tanks were available. Of the tank casualties, combat losses were probably less than 150, arising from the Alytus battle on 22 June, the skirmishes south of Vilnius on 23 June, and the Molodechno counter-attack on 25 June. The remaining 130 tanks were either abandoned or ran out of fuel. There is reasonably good photographic coverage of the Alytus–Vilnius fighting, and German photographs of Soviet tanks show many with no obvious battle damage. This reinforces the conclusion of recent Russian histories that a large percentage of Soviet tank losses in 1941 were due to mechanical problems, road mishaps and fuel shortages. Soviet fuel stocks at the start of the campaign were not generous: about 1.5 days' supply for the 3rd Mechanized Corps. Furthermore, there is some recent evidence that a portion of this fuel stock was not on hand at the unit bases in Lithuania, but in reserve further back in Belarus.

The catastrophic loss rate of the 5th Tank Division was not unusual for the Red Army in the summer of 1941, and some other examples provide a sense of the 1941 calamity. The 12th Tank Division of the 12th Mechanized Corps started the campaign in the Baltic region with 236 BT tanks, but had only nine serviceable BT-7 tanks on 7 July 1941 after only two weeks of fighting. Of the losses, 133 were combat losses and 94 were the result of mechanical breakdowns or accidents. The 7th Mechanized Corps in the Smolensk area had 229 BT tanks at the start of the campaign, reduced to 171 in the first two weeks of fighting. During the subsequent battles of 6–19 July, 143 BT tanks were destroyed, 22 were damaged and only six remained in service in the corps. The Western Front, which started the campaign with 656 BT tanks, had only 101 by 1 October 1941 and only 43 by 28 October. The 24th Tank Division started the war with 141 BT tanks, but had only 34 in service on 1 August after five weeks of fighting on the Leningrad Front. The Leningrad Military District started the campaign with 863 BT tanks; by 27 September it was down to 58 operational BT tanks.

While the loss rate of the Soviet tanks may seem abnormally high, it should be recalled that by 28 June, the numbers of PzKpfw 38(t) tanks in service with 7. Panzer-Division were down to about half their original strength. Combat losses had not been especially high, but there had been many mechanical breakdowns. On 24 July, roughly a month after the start of the campaign, only about 40 per cent of Panzer-Regiment 25's PzKpfw 38(t) tanks were still operational. The critical difference between the German and Soviet experience was that after the border battles, the Wehrmacht controlled the battlefield, so PzKpfw 38(t) tanks that broke down remained in German hands and could be recovered and serviced. Soviet BT-7 tanks that broke down or ran out of fuel remained behind enemy lines and so were total losses.

7. Panzer Division tank strength, 24 July 1941

Type	Strength, 22 June	Total losses	In repair	Operational	% operational
PzKpfw I	17	4	3	10	60
PzKpfw II	55	7	17	31	56
PzKpfw 38(t)	167	34	65	68	40
PzKpfw IV	30	5	12	13	43
PzBefWg	15	3	5	7	47
PzSpWg Panhard	64	34	17	13	20

PzKpfw 38(t) Eastern Front statistics 1941

	May	Jun	Jul	Aug	Sep	Oct	Nov	Dec
Strength*	686	754	763	661	543	547	528	434
Losses	0	33	182	183	62	85	149	102

* As of 1st of each month.

Soviet tank losses in 1941 were staggering. Recent Russian histories of the campaign have labelled it the 'tank massacre of 1941' (*Tankoviy pogrom*). In the border battles in the first three weeks of the campaign, the Red Army lost about 12,000 tanks. Of the 22,000 Soviet tanks that had existed at the outset of Operation *Barbarossa*, there were only 2,200 in front-line service at the beginning of 1942. Total Soviet tank losses in 1941 were about 20,500. In contrast, German tanks losses on the Eastern Front in 1941 were about 3,000, a seven-fold difference. Only a small fraction of these Soviet losses were caused by tank-versus-tank or tank-versus-anti-tank gun engagements. A very large percentage, certainly more than half, were due to the great encirclement battles in which thousands of Soviet tanks were trapped and abandoned.

Soviet tank losses in 1941 by campaign

Operation	Period	Losses
Baltic defensive operation	22 June–9 July 1941	2,523
Belorussian defensive operation	22 June–9 July 1941	4,799
Western Ukraine defensive operation	22 June–6 July 1941	4,381
Karelian operation vs Finland	29 June–10 October 1941	546
Kiev defensive operation	7 July–26 September 1941	411
Leningrad defensive operation	10 July–30 September 1941	1,492
Smolensk operation	10 July–10 September 1941	1,348
Donbas–Rostov defensive operation	29 September–16 November 1941	101
Moscow defensive operation	30 September–5 December 1941	2,785
Tikhvin offensive	10 November–30 December 1941	70

Rostov offensive	17 November–2 December 1941	42
Moscow offensive	5 December 1941–7 January 1942	429
Sub-total (listed campaigns)		*18,927*
Total	**22 June–31 December 1941**	**20,500**

At the time of the commencement of Operation *Barbarossa* in June 1941, the PzKpfw 38(t) equipped five of the 17 Panzer divisions taking part in the invasion of the Soviet Union, or about 20 per cent of the attack force. The PzKpfw 38(t) had battlefield survivability nearly identical to that of the PzKpfw III and PzKpfw IV, with the five Panzer divisions suffering about 27 per cent losses in their PzKpfw 38(t) tanks during June–August 1941. Mines were a particular problem, and 20. Panzer-Division estimated that half of its combat losses of the PzKpfw 38(t) were due to mines. Due to the PzKpfw 38(t)'s smaller size, encounters with mines usually resulted in heavier casualties among drivers and radio operators in the front of the tank compared to larger and heavier tanks such as the PzKpfw IV. One of the main technical problems facing German tank units in the Soviet Union was the sheer distance involved in the advance. Tanks of this era did not have especially great range, and their durability was badly affected by long road-marches in dusty conditions which degraded engine and power-train durability. By late August and early September 1941, the five Panzer divisions employing the PzKpfw 38(t) only had about 58 per cent of their tanks fit for action and the rest in repair. The level of durability of the PzKpfw 38(t) was similar to that of the PzKpfw IV, and somewhat better than the PzKpfw III which continued to suffer from transmission problems.

Durability and losses of German tank types, August–September 1941				
	PzKpfw II	**PzKpfw III**	**PzKpfw IV**	**PzKpfw 38(t)**
Operational (%)	73	48	58	58
In repair (%)	27	52	42	42
Losses (%)	19	28	27	27

A motorcyclist looks over one of the T-28 medium tanks of the 9th Tank Regiment knocked out during the fighting on the east bank of the Neman River near Alytus on 22 June 1941. (NARA)

Total PzKpfw 38(t) losses in 1941 were over 800 tanks out of a starting strength of fewer than 700 at the beginning of Operation *Barbarossa*. In the case of 7. Panzer-Division, of its 151 losses in 1941, 99 were due to enemy action and 52 were due to mechanical breakdown. In the event, 7. Panzer-Division was shipped back to Western Europe for reconstruction in early 1942 and left its PzKpfw 38(t) tanks behind with 1. Panzer-Division and 2. Panzer-Division.

AFTERMATH

The fighting in 1941, and the appearance of the new Soviet T-34 and KV tanks, made it clear that the PzKpfw 38(t) was obsolete. 1. Panzer-Division commented about the PzKpfw 38(t) in April 1942 that 'These Panzers are knocked out by the T-34 at ranges of 200 to 800 meters. The Panzer 38(t) can't destroy or repulse a T-34 at these ranges. Because of its gun, a T-34 can knock out an attacking Panzer at long range.' After 12. Panzer-Division was converted to the PzKpfw III in 1942, this left only three Panzer divisions (8., 19. and 20.) on the Eastern Front with the dwindling number of PzKpfw 38(t) through the spring and summer 1942 campaigns. By the end of 1942, there were only about 300 PzKpfw 38(t) tanks in service and they were gradually retired to secondary roles such as anti-partisan warfare, reconnaissance and training.

Plans to continue PzKpfw 38(t) tank production throughout 1942 were changed and production of the PzKpfw 38(t) Ausf G ended in June 1942. The chassis was too small to accommodate a long 5cm gun or a 7.5cm gun in a turret. Instead, PzKpfw 38(t) production capacity was earmarked for the manufacture of the Marder III tank destroyer, which mounted the new 7.5cm PaK 40 anti-tank gun in a light armoured casemate on top of the hull. While not as versatile as a turreted tank, the Marder III had enough firepower to deal with the emerging Soviet tank threat.

The BT-7 tank became increasingly scarce after 1941. There are no comprehensive statistics for early 1942, but figures available for the summer battles of 1942 suggest that there were only a few hundred still in front-line use in European Russia. By the time of the Stalingrad battles in the autumn and winter of 1942–43, there were hardly any BT tanks still in front-line service. The last known combat use of the BT-7 in European Russia was in the isolated Leningrad region. At the end of the war in 1945, there were only 299 BT tanks of various types in European Russia of which only 43 were in use, mainly for training, with the remainder in the repair plants. The last

reservoir of BT tanks was in the Far East, where three battalions of BT-7 tanks took part in the short war against Japan in August 1945. By the end of September 1945, there were still 190 BT-5 and 1,030 BT-7 tanks in the Far East; all were retired in 1946.

The poor quality of the roads in the Soviet Union contributed to the mechanical difficulties experienced by German tanks in 1941. The sandy and dusty roads led to premature clogging of engine filters and abrasion of mechanical components. This photograph was taken on 9 July 1941 after Panzer-Regiment 25 had crossed the old Soviet frontier into Belarus during its advance on Minsk and the Berezina River. (NARA)

FURTHER READING

Although the battles for Alytus and Vilnius are often covered in general histories of Operation *Barbarossa*, detailed accounts are lacking.

From the German perspective, the *Kriegstagebuch* (KTB: war diary) of 7. Panzer-Division provides an essential skeletal framework of the actions, but offers very little detail about the tank battles. Much of the records of XXXIX. Armeekorps (mot.) were lost and surviving bits in the RG 242 microfilm collection at the National Archives and Records Administration at College Park, Maryland offer little coverage of these battles. Manteuffel's divisional history for this period is heavily based on the KTB; Manteuffel at the time served in one of the division's infantry battalions. Hans von Luck also served in the division at the time, but his memoir lacks details on this battle. Horst Ohrloff, a young PzKpfw 38(t) company commander in Panzer-Regiment 25, provides one of the few detailed accounts from the German perspective in the Glantz study. Otto Carius is better known as a Tiger ace late in the war, but he was an inexperienced young PzKpfw 38(t) loader in 1941, serving in Panzer-Regiment 21 alongside 7. Panzer-Division. Hermann Hoth provides a good assessment of the campaign from a command perspective.

From the Soviet perspective, the Drig study remains the essential history of Soviet mechanized corps in 1941. The recent Ulanov and Shein book focuses on the early combat actions of the T-34 in 1941, and since the 5th Tank Division was one of the first units with this tank, the study provides a good deal of new information. There are scattered bits and pieces about the battle in the many Russian accounts of the 1941 campaign. A four-part series of articles in *Pravda* starting on 22 June 2005 collected a great many of the surviving personal reminiscences. There are no known memoirs from the 5th Tank Division.

Beshanov, Vladimir (2000). *Tankoviy pogrom 1941 goda*. Minsk: Kharvest.

Carius, Otto (1992). *Tigers in the Mud*. Mechanicsburg, PA: Stackpole.

Drig, Evgeniy (2005). *Mekhanizirovannye korpusa RKKA v boyu: istoriya avtobronetankovykh voysk krasnoy armii v 1940-1941 godakh*. Moscow: Tranzitkniga.

Forczyk, Robert (2013). *Tank Warfare on the Eastern Front 1941–42: Schwerpunkt*. Barnsley: Pen & Sword.

Francev, Vladimir & Kliment, Charles (1997). *Praga LT vz. 38*. St. Paul, MN: MBI.

Glantz, David, ed. (1993). *The Initial Period of War on the Eastern Front 22 June–August 1941*. London: Frank Cass.

Hoth, Hermann (2013). *Panzer Operations: Germany's Panzer Group 3 during the Invasion of Russia 1941*. Havertown, PA: Casemate.

Jentz, Thomas & Doyle, Hilary (2007). *Panzerkampfwagen 38(t)*. Boyds, MD: Panzertracts.

Manteuffel, Hasso von (1978). *Die 7. Panzer-Division*. Eggolsheim: Podzun-Pallas.

Manteuffel, Hasso von (1965). *Die 7. Panzer-Division im Zweiten Weltkrieg: Einsatz und Kampf der 'Gespenster-Division' 1939–1945*. Bielefeld: Traditionsverband 7. Panzer-Division.

Pavlov, M, Zhletov, I. & Pavlov, I. (2001). *Tanki BT*. Moscow: Eksprint.

Reese, Roger (1996). *Stalin's Reluctant Soldiers: A Social History of the Red Army 1925–1941*. Lawrence, KS: University Press of Kansas.

Shirokorad, A.B. (2009). *Tankovaya voyna na vostochnom fronte*. Moscow: Veche.

Solyankin, A.G., *et al.* (2002). *Otechestvennye bronirovannye mashiny XX vek: Tom 1: 1905–41*. Moscow: Eksprint.

Solyankin, A.G., *et al.* (2002). *Otechestvennye bronirovannye mashiny XX vek: Tom 2: 1941–45*. Moscow: Eksprint.

Stahel, David (2009). *Operation Barbarossa and Germany's Defeat in the East*. Cambridge: Cambridge University Press.

Ulanov, Andrey & Shein, Dmitriy (2013). *Pervye T-34*. Moscow: Tactical Press.

INDEX

References to illustrations are shown in **bold**.

80